SCHOOLING REDESIGNED

TOWARDS INNOVATIVE LEARNING SYSTEMS

Please cite this publication as:
OECD (2015), *Schooling Redesigned: Towards Innovative Learning Systems*, Educational Research and Innovation, OECD Publishing, Paris.
http://dx.doi.org/10.1787/9789264245914-en

ISBN 9789264245907 (print)
ISBN 9789264245914 (PDF)

Photo credits:
Cover © Inmagine LTD

Corrigenda to OECD publications may be found on line at: *www.oecd.org/publishing/corrigenda*.

Foreword

The demands on learners and thus education systems are evolving fast. In the past, education was about teaching people something. Now, it is about making sure that individuals develop a reliable compass and the navigation skills to find their own way through an increasingly uncertain, volatile and ambiguous world. These days, we no longer know exactly how things will unfold, often we are surprised and need to learn from the extraordinary, and sometimes we make mistakes along the way. And it will often be the mistakes and failures, when properly understood, that create the context for learning and growth. A generation ago, teachers could expect that what they taught would last for a lifetime of their students. Today, schools need to prepare students for more rapid economic and social change than ever before, for jobs that have not yet been created, to use technologies that have not yet been invented, and to solve social problems that we do not yet know will arise.

How do we foster motivated, engaged learners who are prepared to conquer the unforeseen challenges of tomorrow, not to speak of those of today? The dilemma for educators is that the kind of skills that are easiest to teach and easiest to test are also the skills that are easiest to digitise, automate and outsource. There is no question that state-of-the-art knowledge in a discipline will always remain important. Innovative or creative people generally have specialised skills in a field of knowledge or a practice. And as much as "learning to learn" skills are important, we always learn by learning something. However, educational success is no longer mainly about reproducing content knowledge, but about extrapolating from what we know and applying that knowledge in novel situations. Put simply, the world no longer rewards people just for what they know – Google knows everything – but for what they can do with what they know. Because that is the main differentiator today, education is becoming more about ways of thinking, involving creativity, critical thinking, problem solving and decision making; about ways of working, including communication and collaboration; about tools for working, including the capacity to recognise and exploit the potential of new technologies; and, last but not least, about the social and emotional skills that help people live and work together.

Conventionally our approach to problems was breaking them down into manageable bits and pieces, and then to teach students the techniques to solve them. But today we create value by synthesising the disparate bits. This is about curiosity, open-mindedness, making connections between ideas that previously seemed unrelated, which requires being familiar with and receptive to knowledge in other fields than our own. If we spend our whole life in a silo of a single discipline, we will not gain the imaginative skills to connect the dots where the next invention will come from.

The world is also no longer divided into specialists and generalists. Specialists generally have deep skills and narrow scope, giving them expertise that is recognised by peers but not valued outside their domain. Generalists have broad scope but shallow skills. What counts increasingly are the versatilists who are able to apply depth of skill to a progressively widening scope of situations and experiences, gaining new competencies, building relationships, and assuming new roles. They are capable not only of constantly adapting but also of constantly learning and growing, of positioning themselves and repositioning themselves in a fast changing world.

Perhaps most importantly, in today's schools, students typically learn individually and at the end of the school year, we certify their individual achievements. But the more interdependent the world becomes, the more we rely on great collaborators and orchestrators who are able to join others in life, work and citizenship. Innovation, too, is now rarely the product of individuals working in isolation but an outcome of how we mobilise, share and link knowledge. So schools need to prepare students for a world in which many people need to collaborate with people of diverse cultural origins, and appreciate different ideas, perspectives and values; a world in which people need to decide how to trust and collaborate across such differences; and a world in which their lives will be affected by issues that transcend national boundaries. Expressed differently, schools need to drive a shift from a world where knowledge that is stacked up somewhere depreciating rapidly in value towards a world in which the enriching power of communication and collaborative flows is increasing.

In many schools around the world, teachers and school leaders are working hard to help learners develop these kinds of knowledge, skills and character attributes. And previous OECD research has identified important learning principles that tend to underpin success in such efforts. These include to make learning central, to encourage engagement, and to have schools become the place where students come to understand themselves as learners; to ensure that learning is social and collaborative; to be acutely sensitive to individual differences and to be highly attuned to learners' motivations and the importance of emotions. They also include to be demanding for each learner without excessive overload; to use assessments consistent with these aims, with strong emphasis on formative feedback; and to promote horizontal connectedness across learning activities and subjects, both in and out of school.

And yet, the status quo has many protectors in education, and OECD Teaching and Learning International Survey (TALIS) found that, across participating countries, an average of two-thirds of teachers consider the school where they work essentially an innovation hostile environment. So it is no real surprise that innovative learning environments remain the exception rather than the rule in most education systems.

This publication seeks to address this problem with an extensive analysis of the design principles and conditions that can make innovation and the implementation of the above learning principles systemic. The publication looks at different ways to innovate the pedagogical core. This is about the interplay between the main players of innovative learning (learners, educators, content and learning resources) and the dynamics that connect those elements (pedagogy and formative evaluation, use of time, and the organisation of educators and learners). It then studies the organisational features and leadership principals that support this process systemically, recognising that learning environments and systems do not change by themselves but need strong design with vision and strategy. Last but not least, the publication explores ways for innovative partnerships which are often neglected in education. This recognises that isolation within a world of complex learning systems is to seriously limit potential. A powerful learning environment and learning system will constantly be creating synergies and finding new ways to enhance professional, social and cultural capital with others. They will do this with families and communities, higher education, cultural institutions, businesses, and especially other schools and learning environments.

The work underpinning this publication has been realised by three interrelated strands. They include research about the fundamentals of learning using international expert knowledge; the study of a range of innovative cases across many countries and education systems; and the search for effective practices for change management and policy implementation. The rationale behind this approach has been the conviction of: the need to ground innovative learning environments in knowledge about how people learn and the circumstances in which they do this most powerfully; the need to understand in detail and to be inspired by actual learning environments; and the need to move beyond the level of individual cases to deepen understanding of how to grow, scale and sustain innovative practice.

Some will call for a robust scientific evidence base to support these strands and to distinguish what is truly innovative and effective from what is simply different. That remains a challenge. The kind of scientific data developed for education has always been better at predicting the past than for designing the future and many non-traditional learning environments have not been good at incorporating systematic study and research into their practices. The report therefore avoids references to "proven" or "best" practices and its principal approach has been to seek broad agreement among the large number of individuals and constituencies involved in this project on what is promising in terms of policy and practice.

The publication was prepared by OECD Directorate for Education and Skills, with David Istance as principal author. Mariana Martínez Salgado was responsible for liaising with the participating education systems and experts and also provided advice on project direction and on the report. Emily Heppner has been responsible for administration and handled the logistics.

Andreas Schleicher,
Director for Education and Skills

Acknowledgements

Many have contributed to this volume. It would not have been possible without much careful work done in the different systems that submitted reports. We extend thanks especially to the ILE system co-ordinators who have led and co-ordinated project activities in their different home settings. We wish to acknowledge those in each system who produced the ILE System Notes and Monitoring Notes, those directly involved from the strategies and initiatives in question, and the "in-kind" support given and on which the ILE project has depended.

Five systems stepped forward to engage in ILE as "Laboratories of Learning Change" on which dedicated workshops were held in Paris in July 2013 and June 2014. We are especially appreciative of these volunteer systems for their close active engagement in this international network:

- *Belgium (French Community)*, with special thanks to Gaëlle Chapelle and Jean-Luc Adams.
- *Canada (British Columbia)*, with special thanks to Judy Halbert and Linda Kaser.
- *New Zealand*, with special thanks to Brian Annan, Rose Carpenter and Jackie Talbot.
- *Peru (Innova Schools)*, with special thanks to Maria Teresa Moreno Alcazar, Jorge Yzusqui Chessman and Gonzalo Conti Perochena.
- *South Africa (KwaZulu-Natal)*, with special thanks to Lynn van der Elst, Edward Mosuwe, Chris Ramdas and Claude Tshimanika.

There were a number of events that contributed importantly to the "Implementation and Change" strand of the ILE project that has resulted in this report. We are particularly grateful for the expert facilitation and wise guidance provided throughout these events by Valerie Hannon and Tony Mackay.

The international conference on ILE took place in Santiago, Chile on 7-9 January 2013, co-organised with the Chilean Ministry of Education, which inter alia discussed implementation and change; particular thanks are extended to Francisco Lagos Marín and Eliana Chamizo Álvarez.

The conference held in Barcelona 3-5 December 2013 was primarily focused on learning leadership but it also contributed to the reflections incorporated in this volume. Particular acknowledgement is due of the support of the Jaume Bofill Foundation, with thanks especially to Ismael Palacín, Anna Jolonch, and Valtencir Mendes.

The ILE seminar on evaluation and innovation held in Paris on 20 June 2014 sought to deepen understanding of a key issue for implementation and change and was well attended by the ILE network. Special thanks go to the experts who prepared the main discussion paper, Lorna Earl and Helen Timperley.

ILE featured prominently in a major conference on "Innovation, Governance and Reform in Education" held in Paris on 3-5 November 2014 to which several CERI projects contributed. This helped to distil arguments that are found in this volume and we wish to acknowledge in particular the roles played in that event by Lucie Cerna and Emily Heppner.

A policy conference took place in London in January 2015 to discuss the first edition of a new OECD flagship publication – "Education Policy Outlook". ILE contributed a chapter to this report and the conference included a workshop on implementing innovative learning environments.

The conference "Building Future Learning Systems: From Exceptional Innovation to Systemic Transformation", jointly organised by the Global Education Leaders' Partnership (GELP), KwaZulu-Natal (South Africa) and OECD/ILE, and held on 19-21 April 2015, discussed the first draft of this report and gave valuable feedback. We wish to thank all involved in organising that conference.

Beyond the ILE co-ordinators, various experts have provided input and feedback to drafts of this report. We extend particular thanks to: Francisco Benavides, Lorna Earl, Valerie Hannon, Tony Mackay, Louise Stoll, Dahle Suggett, and Helen Timperley. Mariana Martínez Salgado has continued to provide invaluable advice and input after having left the OECD staff at the end of 2014.

We also wish to acknowledge the support and helpful input from members of the CERI Governing Board and CERI staff. Within the OECD Secretariat, Janina Cuevas Zuniga and Stephanie Villalobos also worked on ILE during this final phase. We wish to thank our colleagues in the EDU Communications and PAC teams, especially Sophie Limoges and Anne-Lise Prigent, for their helpful inputs, and all other colleagues who have given their support. The layout was undertaken by Design Media.

Table of contents

Figures

Boxes

Executive summary

The question of how well education systems develop knowledge, skills and capacities, and of what kinds, is increasingly centre stage in public debate. It represents a different starting point for innovation compared with the longstanding progressive ambition to realise more holistic educational opportunities and promote individual development. Yet, both call for innovation and for systemic change, not isolated innovation here and there. Innovating learning environments with collaborative definitions of professionalism and the strong engagement of all partners (most especially young people themselves) are also more likely to enhance the attractiveness of teaching than backward-looking definitions.

Among other factors, the penetration of digital technologies and the extent of global connection, the entry of new learning providers, the interest of employers in the outcomes of schooling and the expertise in learning in other sectors (e.g. in the creative sector), and the extent of networking have made the vertical conception of school systems increasingly partial.

The ILE project began with the need for terms and concepts defined in terms of learning, not the formal institutional system of schooling. One basic concept adopted in this report is that of "learning eco-systems" – interdependent combinations of different species of providers and organisations playing different roles with learners in differing relationships to them over time and in varying mixes. As regards levels, we use the following conceptual distinctions:

- *The "learning environment" (micro) level* as conceptualised in earlier ILE work. It is neutral about the institutional arrangements underpinning it, though many learning environments are located in schools.
- *The "meso" level* as comprised of the many compounds of learning environments in networks, communities, chains and initiatives. This is critical for growing, diffusing and sustaining innovative learning.
- *The "meta" level* as the aggregation of all the learning environments and connected arrangements that come within the boundaries chosen.

ILE has developed the "7+3" framework, referring to the seven learning principles and the three dimensions of innovative organisation. This report has extended that framework by embracing the nature of networks and strategies at the meso level, to ask:

- *Learning focused:* How learning focused is the network or strategy and how is this understood? This is about aims and the centrality of learning.
- *Balance of formal and non-formal:* How much in evidence are non-formal learning providers, whether as alternatives or in mixed combinations with schools? How networked are formal learning environments in non-formal ways? This is about who is involved.

- *Learning and network diffusion:* How do the meso-level strategies and networks actually spread learning innovation? This is about diffusion within networked learning systems.

In its third strand on "Implementation and Change", the ILE study invited systems to participate through submitting particular strategies or initiatives for innovating learning beyond single schools or organisations. The design features running through them can be summarised as a series of "Cs":

- *Culture change:* Several of the strategies emphasise the importance of creating culture change in schools as more important than surface change but also much more difficult to realise.

- *Clarifying focus:* Clear focus and prioritising are essential, as trying to cover everything all at once risks disjointed diffusion of effort and of missing all targets in the process.

- *Capacity creation – knowledge and professional learning:* A common cornerstone is the need to generate knowledge about the learning that is taking place, and for that knowledge to be acted upon. This means widespread professional learning and thereby capacity creation.

- *Collaboration and co-operation:* Collaborative professionalism is assumed in many of the strategies just as networks and professional learning communities are based on collaboration and co-operation.

- *Communication technologies and platforms:* Platforms and digital communications have become a prominent part of strategies to grow and sustain innovative learning environments.

- *Change agents:* A number of the strategies involve the creation of specific change agents; they may be supported by specialist institutes as well.

Growing and sustaining innovative learning at scale needs to be located in an understanding of the *complexity* of contemporary learning systems with many settings, players and connections. The creation of flourishing networked learning eco-systems (the meso level) is a principal means for broader meta transformation to occur.

Given the importance of relationships and connectors, *knowledge* is a critical part of the dynamics of system change and evaluative knowledge an integral aspect of innovation and implementation. Theories of change are needed to connect actions, strategies and policies with the intended beneficial results. Narratives can be invaluable for translating theories of change into actionable agendas.

Relationships, connections and trust take *time* to build and play out; the interaction of networks and communities unfold in time; it takes time to learn, whether by individuals, classes, schools, networks, communities of practice, districts, stakeholders, or ministries of education. Several of the featured strategies used pilots; some have preferred rapid prototyping, working to much shorter time frames.

The issue of leadership in such complex systems becomes critical and increasingly challenging. Often leadership will come from new players, outside the traditional system. But government leadership remains important including in generating coherence of aims, infrastructure and accountability. Governments have a privileged role to play in: i) regulating, ii) incentivising, and iii) accelerating.

When these are in place, a meta learning eco-system that has thoroughly integrated the ILE framework will have:

- high learning activity and motivation levels, with prominent learner agency and voice

- educators who are active, collaborating and highly knowledgeable about learning

- a rich mix and diversity of pedagogical practices with highly visible personalised approaches, active pedagogies and formative assessment
- extensive inter-disciplinarity, curriculum development and new learning materials
- widespread innovative applications of digital resources and social media
- cultures of using learning evidence and evaluation, including sophisticated information systems
- flourishing new evaluation and assessment metrics
- highly visible, diverse partners involved in education
- a thriving, vibrant meso level
- dense global connections well beyond traditional system and geographical boundaries.

Chapter 1

The challenge of transformation towards innovative learning systems

This chapter introduces the rationale and key concepts used in the report, and summarises its main findings and arguments. The growing fact and understanding of complexity in learning systems highlights the impoverishment of mechanical metaphors and the assumption of policy omnipotence within well-defined systems. Organic concepts and models are needed: learning eco-systems, which can be understood as divided into the learning environment (micro) level, the "meso" networked level, and the overall "meta" level. This report analyses the submitted networked initiatives in terms of whether and in what way they are learning focused, what is the balance they achieve of formal and non-formal, and their means of diffusion. The shared features of the strategies and initiatives are summarised as a series of "Cs": Culture change, Clarifying focus, Capacity creation, knowledge and professional learning, Collaboration and co-operation, Communication technologies and platforms, and Change agents. The creation of flourishing networked learning eco-systems is a principal means for broader meta transformation to occur. This chapter focuses especially on knowledge, time and leadership, including the role of government.

The innovation imperative

Education has become increasingly important worldwide, and consequently so has its star risen in the political constellation. A (possibly *the*) key driver for this is economic – the fundamental role identified of knowledge, skills and capacities to underpin and maintain prosperity. The question of how well education systems develop knowledge, skills and capacities, and of what kinds, is increasingly centre stage in public debate. No argument has more political purchase today regarding education's value than that it enhances competitiveness, even if competition by definition has winners and losers and even if pursuit of competitive edge may come into tension with the array of other missions with which education is charged.

The direct link to international competitiveness, and the fact of globalisation, means that education's international dimension has grown markedly over at least the past two decades. It is both cause and effect – global interdependence has fuelled comparative measurements and they in turn fuel the thirst for more. It also renders education more complex, given the range of cross-border educational activities and the prominent international benchmarks that have become so influential nationally and locally.

These developments create an intense pressure for reform. In many quarters, this is seen as the need to modernise and innovate bureaucratic school systems in their methods, content, etc. To this are added the severe pressures on public spending which put the spotlight on perceived inefficiencies. The pressure often takes the form of favouring "learning" over "education", and signals a readiness to disrupt accepted institutional arrangements as too slow to change, too inward-looking and too detached from the rapid economic shifts taking place globally and locally. It is an argument for radical overhaul of learning environments at scale, including, in the language of the OECD schooling scenarios (OECD, 2001), "de-schooling".

It represents a very different starting point for innovation compared with the longstanding educational/progressive desire to realise more holistic educational opportunities and promote individual development. On this view, the problem is not that the institutions of education are too detached from the economy but that they are too close, and are pulled to narrow their curricula and instil only superficial knowledge and not deep understanding. The charge is also that education systems are profoundly inequitable, far too driven by the social and economic function of sorting and selecting, and thus not organised for the optimisation of learning. In the language of the OECD schooling scenarios, this is an argument for "re-schooling".

The economic critique and the educational critique may thus seem poles apart. But in other respects, they come closely into alignment and make the pressure to innovate so strong because such divergent starting points lead to the same basic conclusion. The critics of either colour may point to supporting evidence in the large numbers of young people who are disengaged from learning by the time they reach their teenage years. Both might insist that radical overhaul is needed, not minor improvements. Both call for innovation and the urgency of enhancing the power of schools and other places to generate learning. Both may say that systemic change is needed, not isolated innovation here and there. Indeed, what may look at first sight to be divergent critiques may turn out to be convergence around different points of emphasis.

Another key constituency are teachers, who work in complex, knowledge-intensive situations and yet in most countries feel that theirs is an ambiguous status with insufficient recognition of their professionalism. One response they can make is to retreat into defensive mode and seek to protect an understanding of professional autonomy as the right of the individual teacher to be left undisturbed in his or her own classroom. Innovating learning environments with collaborative definitions of professionalism and the strong engagement of all partners (and most especially young people themselves) offers a far more promising route for enhancing the attractiveness of teaching than such backward-looking definitions of professionalism.

The differences of the critiques and constituencies notwithstanding, they coalesce around the urgent need to innovate the fundamentals of schooling. If schools are to make serious inroads towards 21st century skills development or towards holistic education or to be highly attractive contemporary professional working environments, it means radical changes to core habits and practices in most schools and systems, where those habits are the residues of the predictability and control practices that resemble little of what a learning organisation is now understood to be (OECD, 2010). It means addressing the low visibility of teacher work and their isolation in highly fragmented classroom arrangements, low engagement of too many of the main players (especially students), conformity and reproduction.

In moving away from excessively bureaucratic models, the growing understanding of complexity highlights the impoverishment of mechanical policy metaphors and the assumption of central policy omnipotence within well-defined and controllable "systems". These fit badly a world of multiple actors, in which global and local players are influential as are non-formal players and activity. Digital connection has transformed communication and boundaries. More organic metaphors and models might seem messy and unpredictable, but eco-systems and complexity have become the nature of the contemporary world. We cannot keep faith with old models simply because they are neater. This understanding runs through this report.

Rethinking systems and levels

With the focus on learning systems and innovation, many conventional frameworks are inadequate by themselves. A conventional assumption is that policy is set by governments and descends in a vertical implementation line through local government together with implementation/support agencies through to school principals and into the classroom. "Learning" and "education" are taken as synonymous with formal schooling. Additional organisations, such as education publishers, examination boards and teacher training organisations are seen as extensions to arrangements set by governments. Yet, these frameworks are increasingly inadequate, if they ever were adequate in the first place. A perennial challenge for policy is that it is notoriously impotent to change behaviour in teaching and learning. Learning systems extend well beyond schools. Innovation means looking beyond the conventional partners and structures.

Among other factors, the penetration of digital technologies and the extent of global connection, the entry of new learning providers, the interest of employers in the outcomes of schooling and the expertise in learning in other sectors (e.g. in the creative sector), and the extent of networking have turned this official, vertical conception – that never was fully adequate – upside down and have stretched it horizontally. We need models that embrace the horizontal as well as the vertical, the non-formal as well as the formal, the unsponsored collaboration as well as the regulated. It is not about neglecting schools and their organising systems but rather integrating them into more comprehensive concepts and systems.

All this entails that we should be thinking of learning eco-systems – interdependent combinations of different species of providers and organisations playing different roles with learners in differing relationships to them over time and in varying mixes. This also means that there is not a system but many, not a "system level" but a complex series of interlocking systems. And change is about much more than policy, if this is seen as the directed change of the education authorities: this is only one among multiple sources of transformation.

As the formal institutional architecture is not defining "systems" in this report, we cannot use familiar distinctions such as between the classroom level, the school level, the district level and the system level. The ILE project began with the need for terms and concepts defined in terms of learning, not the formal institutional system of schooling. In this report, we apply the following distinctions:

- The *learning environment* (micro) level: This is as conceptualised in previous ILE work. It is neutral about the institutional arrangements underpinning it, though many learning environments are located in schools.
- The *meso* level: Comprised of the many compounds of learning environments in networks, communities, chains and initiatives, this level – which is largely invisible in the formal governance charts of education systems – is critical for growing, diffusing and sustaining innovative learning.
- The *meta* level: The boundaries defining this level might be very widely drawn or more restrictive; it is the aggregation of all the learning environments and meso-level arrangements that come within the system boundaries chosen.

The strategies submitted to the ILE study are primarily examples of meso-level change. These are discussed and analysed in Chapters 3 and 4. Wider meta-level change is discussed in Chapters 2 and 5.

Extending the ILE framework

Developing a framework to understand learning environments and systems has been one of the primary aims and outcomes of the ILE international study. The framework presented in the volume *Innovative Learning Environments* (OECD, 2013) we dubbed "7+3" because it was built around the seven design principles and the three dimensions overlaying them. These are presented briefly below. This volume has extended this framework in two ways. First, it has elaborated (Chapter 2) the implications of the 7+3 framework for the conditions and policies that would promote it, and outlines indicators that would show when the ILE framework is becoming the norm. Second, it extends the framework to make it appropriate for understanding learning systems.

The seven learning principles

The 7 of the 7+3 are the seven essential design principles identified in *The Nature of Learning* report (Dumont, Istance and Benavides, 2010). These principles originally referred to the design of individual learning environments so as to optimise learning. But they equally serve as principles to guide wider strategies, reforms and system change. In order to be most effective, schools and other learning environments should attend to all of the following design principles:

- *Learning Principle One:* Make learning central, encourage engagement, and be where learners come to understand themselves as learners.
- *Learning Principle Two:* Ensure that learning is social and often collaborative.
- *Learning Principle Three:* Be highly attuned to learners' motivations and the importance of emotions.
- *Learning Principle Four:* Be acutely sensitive to individual differences including in prior knowledge.
- *Learning Principle Five:* Be demanding for each learner but without excessive overload.
- *Learning Principle Six:* Use assessments consistent with these aims, with strong emphasis on formative feedback.
- *Learning Principle Seven:* Promote horizontal connectedness across learning activities and subjects, in- and out-of-school.

The three innovation dimensions

The follow-up ILE report *Innovative Learning Environments* (OECD, 2013) maintained the learning principles as fundamental to all activities and organisation but then added three more dimensions to optimise the conditions for putting the principles into practice:

i. *Innovate the pedagogical core.* This is about ensuring that the core aims, practices and dynamics are innovated to match the ambition of the learning principles. It is about innovating both the core *elements* (learners, educators, content and learning resources) and the *dynamics* that connect those elements (pedagogy and formative evaluation, use of time, and the organisation of educators and learners).

ii. *Become "formative organisations" with strong learning leadership.* Learning environments and systems do not just change by themselves but need strong design with vision and strategies. To be firmly focused on learning such leadership needs to be constantly informed by self-review and evidence on learning achieved.

iii. *Open up to partnerships.* This recognises that isolation within a world of complex learning systems is to seriously limit potential. A powerful learning environment and learning system will constantly be creating synergies and finding new ways to enhance professional, social and cultural capital with others. They will do this with families and communities, higher education, cultural institutions, businesses, and especially other schools and learning environments.

Extending the ILE learning architecture

The above ILE framework is "institution-neutral" as the learning environment as we have defined it may be found in a wide variety of different institutional forms. But in describing the architecture of learning eco-systems, we need to be able to distinguish different organisational arrangements and characterise the kind of learning system it is. This report extends the ILE framework to embrace the nature of networks and strategies at the meso level.

Learning focused: How learning focused is the network, and how far focused on innovative learning as defined in ILE work through the seven principles? This is about aims and the centrality of learning. The strategies and initiatives submitted to the ILE study by definition are already biased towards growing innovative learning but many different approaches can be seen. Several of the networked initiatives stand out by giving importance to scanning and identifying the learning challenge at the outset, rather than this being taken as known. They tend to privilege the role played by learners and their families in this process and adopt variants around 21st century competences to define their learning aims. But some also emphasise knowledge of traditional cultural values.

Balance of formal and non-formal: How much in evidence are non-formal learning providers, whether as alternatives to or in mixed combinations with schools? How networked are formal learning environments in non-formal ways? At one end of the spectrum are the formal clusters of schools. Less formal is when different schools or communities of practice come together in voluntary ways. There may be purely non-formal bodies or initiatives not operating through school institutions at all. Mapping all the different elements of the meta learning system means to capture its horizontality as well as the basic vertical structures of the school system.

The means of innovation "contagion": How do the meso strategies and networks actually spread learning innovation? This is about the nature of the connections for diffusion within networked learning systems. The featured strategies rely on a wide variety of different methods to connect and diffuse innovation. One problem to be encountered is when strategies become "victims of their own success" and the desired volume of exchange outstrips capacity.

Common features of the ILE strategies and initiatives

The ILE study invited systems to participate in its third strand through submitting particular strategies or initiatives for innovating learning beyond single schools or organisations. About 25 systems (countries, regions, networks) chose to participate. The initiatives and strategies submitted to the ILE project are populating the meso level of their broader eco-systems of learning by creating different networks, chains and communities to lead and diffuse innovation. Their submissions should not be understood as "best practices", though they may well inspire others. As networks and initiatives are constantly emerging and evolving, they often disappear as well: growing innovative learning systems depends on the emergence of new learning-focused networked initiatives outstripping the inevitable decline or disappearance of others.

The design features that run through these diverse strategies and initiatives may be summarised as a series of headings, each beginning with the letter "C":

- ***Culture change:*** Several of the strategies emphasise the importance of creating culture change in schools being more important than surface change but also much more difficult to realise.
- ***Clarifying focus:*** Many of the innovation strategies are aimed right at such mainstream goals as addressing low educational achievement and enhancing quality. Innovation is necessary because repeating variants of conventional approaches fail to make a significant difference. Clear focus is the opposite of "letting 1 000 flowers bloom". Trying to cover everything all at once risks disjointed diffusion of effort and of missing all targets in the process.
- ***Capacity creation – knowledge and professional learning:*** A common cornerstone of the submissions is the need to generate knowledge about the learning that is taking place, and for that knowledge to be acted upon. This means professional learning and thereby capacity creation. They go hand-in-hand with knowledge enhancement and often a research component is needed to understand how a strategy might be optimised and to create the materials to do so.
- ***Collaboration and co-operation:*** Collaborative professionalism is assumed in many of the strategies just as networks and professional learning communities are based on collaboration and co-operation. Networking is becoming the natural form of collective action in contemporary learning systems. There is a clear policy role in helping to establish the climate and means for effective networking.
- ***Communication technologies and platforms:*** Platforms and digital communications have become a prominent part of strategies to grow and sustain innovative learning environments, while taking many different forms.
- ***Change agents:*** A number of the strategies involve the creation through policy initiatives of specific change agents, who are able to exercise influence on the ground and provide the expertise and drive to sustain the innovation. They may be supported by specialist institutes as well.

Transforming learning systems

Growing and sustaining innovative learning at scale needs to be located in an understanding of the complexity of contemporary learning systems with many settings, players and connections. The creation of flourishing sets of meso networked learning eco-systems is a principal means through which the broader meta transformation can take place.

Given the importance of relationships and connectors, *knowledge* is a critical part of the dynamics of the innovation process and learning architecture. The relevant concept of knowledge is very broad and includes both codified and tacit knowledge. Evaluative knowledge is not something apart that comes along afterwards to assess impact: it is an integral aspect of innovation and implementation. Participants are thereby empowered to take informed leadership decisions and to engage in design constantly informed by evaluative thinking.

Theories of change are needed to connect actions, strategies and policies with the intended beneficial results. They provide the maps to help steer change and engage different stakeholders with common purpose. Even having a theory of change is not enough as there needs to be an understanding and capacity to actually bring those changes about. *Narratives* can be invaluable for translating theories of change into actionable agendas. They give the different players a sense of direction and the reasons why change itself is important.

Relationships, connections and trust take time; the interaction of networks and communities unfold in time; it takes time to learn, no matter who is doing the learning – individuals, classes, schools, networks, communities of practice, districts, stakeholders, or ministries of education. Several of the featured strategies were implemented through pilots, so giving time to learn about processes before going to larger scale. But often the term "pilot" is used to refer to relatively small-scale initiatives without the serious intention that they will ever lead to wider adoption. Some have preferred rapid prototyping, working to much shorter time frames.

The issue of *leadership* in such complex systems becomes critical and increasingly challenging. Often leadership will come from new players, outside the traditional system. But government leadership remains important and its legitimacy, breadth and capacity to unlock resources often make it central to the change process. The overall structure and distribution of learning opportunities is an area where government has an especially important role to play, in seeking to generate coherence of aims, infrastructure and accountability. Among the strategic options for government action, they have a privileged role in: i) regulating; ii) incentivising; and iii) accelerating.

Systems transformed

What will learning systems exhibiting high adherence to the ILE framework look like? This profile description draws on the indicators developed in Chapter 2 that would show that a meta system had developed along ILE lines. Such systems will demonstrate particular profiles of attitudes and learning engagement, whether referring to young people or to the adults active within the learning system. There will be high levels of engagement and persistence by learners, and schools and classrooms will be characterised by the "buzz" of collegial activity and learning. They will also be characterised by very active learner voice and agency. This is not just in places called "schools": a wide variety of sites for learning will be commonplace beyond conventional classrooms, more or less integrated into school organisations.

There will have been a matching shift in educator views, knowledge and practice. Teachers and other educators spend significant time engaged in professional discussion about learning strategies in general, within the organisation and in relation to individual learners. They engage readily with learning leadership, innovation and professional collaboration, including team teaching. They are familiar with the ILE Learning Principles and diverse teaching strategies related to them. System-wide there will be a rich mix and diversity of pedagogical practices, with personalised approaches and formative assessment highly visible.

There is widespread use of social media and ICT, as learners engage in research and intense exchanges around learning projects and educators connect with each other, with learners, and with other partners and networks. Teaching, learning and pedagogy are often tech-rich. There has been extensive work on integrating interdisciplinary knowledge around key concepts and developing corresponding learning materials and pedagogies. There is flourishing research and development around pedagogical expertise and integrated content knowledge.

There is a dominant culture and practice of evaluative thinking and self-review and of using evaluative evidence formatively to inform design strategies. Leadership is shared and strongly focused on learning and design. Partners who previously might have been regarded as external have become integral to learning systems, importantly including families, community bodies, enterprises, cultural institutions, universities, foundations, and other learning environments. Information systems are highly developed to permit the detailed learning information to be readily accessible for all engaged in designing the teaching strategies and the learning environment.

Flourishing new metrics have been developed to assess learning and in widespread use. These reflect the aims of learning environments and wider system metrics, and include mastery, understanding, the capacity to transfer and use knowledge, curiosity, creativity, teamwork and persistence. Assessment extends outside conventional school settings. Quality assurance systems, including inspection, recognise successful learner engagement and exercise of voice.

High levels of collaboration and engagement with partners, including other learning environments, will mean the highly visible, dense meso-level arrangements across districts, networks, chains, and communities of practice, whether formed spontaneously or through formalised strategies and networking initiatives. Non-formal education providers feature prominently. In a global world, it is common practice that partnership contacts, with other learning environments and different stakeholders, extend beyond national boundaries.

References

Dumont, H., D. Istance, and F. Benavides (eds) (2010), *The Nature of Learning: Using Research to Inspire Practice*, Educational Research and Innovation, OECD Publishing, Paris, http://dx.doi.org/10.1787/9789264086487-en.

OECD (2013), *Innovative Learning Environments*, Educational Research and Innovation, OECD Publishing, Paris, http://dx.doi.org/10.1787/9789264203488-en.

OECD (2010), *Innovative Workplaces: Making Better Use of Skills within Organisations*, Educational Research and Innovation, OECD Publishing, Paris, http://dx.doi.org/10.1787/9789264095687-en.

OECD (2001), *What Schools for the Future?*, Educational Research and Innovation, OECD Publishing, Paris, http://dx.doi.org/10.1787/9789264195004-en.

Chapter 2

Conditions and signposts in generalising innovative learning environments

This chapter extends the 7+3 framework developed in earlier ILE analyses by examining the conditions and policies that will be conducive to making the framework widespread practice. It summarises these under the following headings: reducing standardisation, fostering innovation, broadening institutions; appropriate accountability and metrics for 21st century learning; fostering learning leadership, trust and learner agency; widespread collaborative expert professionalism; ubiquitous professional learning; connectivity and extensive digital infrastructure; flourishing cultures of networks and partnership; and powerful knowledge systems and cultures of evaluation. The chapter extends the framework further by offering signposts to show when indeed it is becoming widespread practice. This is done by examining each of the ten elements of the framework and presenting indicators that would show whether each has become typical. The chapter concludes with a condensed set of such indicators.

This chapter reiterates the full framework of the powerful innovative learning environment as developed in the OECD/CERI study (OECD 2013). But it takes it further in looking at how it might be extended as widespread practice. Instead of asking simply "what does a powerful and innovative learning environment look like?", it asks and develops responses to two further questions:

- *Conditions and policies:* What kinds of broader changes and conditions will be needed to help ensure that these design principles become commonplace features of learning systems?
- *Indicators:* What will we expect to see as revealing that the framework and its features have become widespread and not simply found in exceptional individual cases?

The focus is thus not on specific policies and initiatives but it is on the larger direction to be travelled. The changes identified are partly about policy in the conventional sense, partly about other means of change and transformation that involve the range of stakeholders and the different system levels. It is as much about climates and conditions as about directed policy. For the indicators of its widespread application, these are identified for each of the ten (7+3) components, and then summarised into a single indicator set at the end.

The ILE 7+3 framework

The 7 of the 7+3 are the identified seven essential design principles identified in *The Nature of Learning* report (Dumont, Istance and Benavides, 2010). Implementing these research-based principles adds up to an agenda of significant change in most contexts if they are to be embedded into daily practice. More demanding still, *all* the principles should be worked towards rather than a selected few. These principles were originally identified in reference to the design of individual learning environments so as to optimise learning. But they equally serve as principles to guide wider strategies, reforms and system change.

Box 2.1. **The ILE "Learning Principles"**

The research-based learning principles state that, in order to be most effective, schools and other learning environments should attend to all of the following design principles:

- *Learning Principle One:* Make learning central, encourage engagement, and be where learners come to understand themselves as learners.
- *Learning Principle Two:* Ensure that learning is social and often collaborative.
- *Learning Principle Three:* Be highly attuned to learners' motivations and the importance of emotions.
- *Learning Principle Four:* Be acutely sensitive to individual differences including in prior knowledge.
- *Learning Principle Five:* Be demanding for each learner but without excessive overload.
- *Learning Principle Six:* Use assessments consistent with these aims, with strong emphasis on formative feedback.
- *Learning Principle Seven:* Promote horizontal connectedness across learning activities and subjects, in- and out-of-school.

The follow-up ILE report *Innovative Learning Environments* (2013) maintained the centrality of the learning principles but then added three more dimensions that are about defining and organising learning environments so that they become powerful and innovative and put the principles into practice. Such powerful learning environments:

- *innovate their pedagogical core* – both the core *elements* (learners, educators, content and learning resources) and the dynamics that connect those elements (pedagogy and formative evaluation, use of time, and the organisation of educators and learners)

- *become "formative organisations" with strong learning leadership* – with vision, strategies and design, all closely informed by self-review and evidence on learning
- *open up to partnerships*, to create synergies and enhance professional, social and cultural capital – with families and communities, higher education, cultural institutions, businesses, and especially other schools and learning environments.

The 7+3 framework is thus based on learning research and the analysis of the innovative cases submitted through the OECD/ILE project. Running right through the framework are the learning principles that emerged from the project's review of learning research (Dumont, Istance and Benavides, 2010).

Conditions and policies for implementing the ILE framework

Reading across the ten different components of the ILE framework, there are directions for change that are consistent with the framework, and indeed actively promote it when they have the right context and interactions with other policies and conditions. This is a first examination, and the appropriate meso- and meta-level changes are further examined later in this volume, through the experiences of the submitted strategies and initiatives, in Chapters 4 and 5.

Reducing standardisation, fostering innovation, broadening institutions

Learning systems should shift away from standardisation while informed by shared general goals for education and learning. All educational institutions and organisations should be strongly focused on the promotion of learning – as activity, as engagement and as successful accomplishment – using demanding notions of "success". Educational policy making has to be, so far as possible, long term and protective of achievements already attained rather than constantly changing in response to short-term demands.

School and system policies need to ensure that institutional functioning and regulation are seen less as ends in themselves but instead constantly and consistently refer to student learning as their essential mission and purpose. Standard rules and uniform procedures should not stymie creative solutions and innovation at the heart of teaching and learning. Regulatory constraints need at least to be re-examined, including bringing partners, experts and volunteers right into activities in the pedagogical cores.

Broadening the institutional base beyond schools through service learning, diverse non-formal learning opportunities on line and in communities, and establishing hybrid formal/non-formal programmes are all part of creating dynamic learning systems. This should be about creating more high-quality opportunities for learners and extending professionalism, leadership and quality assurance; it is not about extending bureaucratic control.

There is a case for extending specialist educational offers. There could well be a rich diversity of different types of school emerging, each with particular ethos and curriculum focus.

Appropriate accountability and metrics for 21st century learning

There needs to be a strong lead towards innovative learning from curriculum and assessment policy. Accountability systems should be cast in terms of a full range of learning aims, methodologies and metrics. Promoting coherence should be a constant aim to avoid competing, self-negating policy strategies and messages. As regards accountability and assessment regimes, they should not be creating highly risk-averse schools just when schools need to be hubs of innovation.

For both systems and individual learning environments, assessments must be used in the service of deep learning and to promote 21st century competences, with close attention to social and emotional skills. There needs to be advances in assessment methodologies including the metrics used. Roadmaps and consumer guides may usefully help access and interpret the wealth of accountability information.

Promoting learning leadership, trust and learner agency

Leadership is critical. This means learning leadership based on deep knowledge of the nature of teaching and learning, and a readiness to innovate and to take calculated risks. It means having the leadership capacity to take staffs, parents and communities forward even on long-term change journeys. It means being able to manage the complex organisational environment of creating visibility and breaking down high boundaries that divide classrooms, schools and communities from each other. All these capacities need to be actively developed and maintained.

Policy frameworks are highly influential of prevailing assumptions. They should move away from the single "heroic" leadership paradigm, and recognise the distributed, shared nature of leadership. There needs to be widespread official acceptance that learners deserve and are able to be active partners in their own educational organisation and decision making. This demands high-trust environments, built around the active engagement of learners, their families and their wider communities (Cerna, 2014).

New leadership and governance arrangements must increasingly recognise complex learning systems and optimise potential opportunities by extending beyond schools themselves. Greater connectedness with partners and networks outside the formal system places greater demands on leadership. A policy role is to encourage the sharing of examples and sponsoring of these complex features of contemporary learning systems.

Widespread collaborative expert professionalism

The ILE framework assumes collaborative professionalism, strongly focused on enhancing learning with a range of partners. Innovating learning environments and embedding this form of professionalism are among the most powerful ways of enhancing the attractiveness of the teaching profession. Teacher professional bodies, unions and associations would very helpfully promote this perspective on professionalism.

There will need to be flexibility in educational cultures, practices and learning spaces, and the capacity to accommodate different pedagogies and mixes of group and individual learning. There needs to be expertise in fostering learner engagement and in making connections between subjects, in- and out-of-school learning, and connecting specific learning tasks to broader concepts and problems; and to be able to do all this collaboratively. These have far-reaching implications for teacher pedagogical knowledge.

Broadening the educator base by bringing others beyond the established teaching force can facilitate connectedness to expertise and experience. At the same time, to do so brings to the fore the leadership and management roles of teachers and school leaders in more complex organisational arrangements.

Ubiquitous professional learning

Learning is needed to build the professional, innovative and organisational capacity to realise the ILE Learning Principles, based on sound design strategy and evaluative thinking, and engaging the learning environment as a whole.

Learning is key to building capacity for distributed leadership formatively exercised using learning evidence; it calls for widespread leadership development opportunities. There should similarly be widespread professional development opportunities in evaluation and evaluative thinking. These may come through collaboration and networking, or specifically organised around leadership programmes and bringing in specialist expertise.

Professional collaboration and exchange should be recognised and incentivised in accountability systems, internal and external. The real and virtual environments inhabited by educators should be highly conducive to professional exchange and dialogue. Policy can foster learner-centred networks and communities of learning.

Connectivity and extensive digital infrastructure

There is a clear policy role for investing and partnering in establishing the necessary digital infrastructure to underpin teaching and learning activities and the extensive knowledge base and curricula involved. It will be important that learning environments are strongly interconnected using digital technology, that they have online visibility to enable the approach of different potential partners, and so that partnerships themselves can communicate easily at a distance on line and using social media.

Flourishing cultures of networking and partnership

Horizontal connection and collaboration should become as normal a way to characterise learning systems as the vertical, formal relations between levels. Education authorities themselves may be very active in establishing networks or brokering communities of practice.

Extending the capacity of learning environments through partnerships will not work if there are high school walls intended to demarcate very clear boundaries between the internal world of the school and various external bodies and stakeholders, especially communities and families, and other learning environments. This bridging is not just about bringing parents and the community more closely into schools; it is also about bringing schools and schooling more into communities.

Connection to such a wide range of potential partners calls for well-organised information about those partners, schools and learning organisations so that they can find each other and work together. Brokers may well be involved, especially around particular themes or about particular networks.

Powerful knowledge systems and cultures of evaluation

Very powerful knowledge systems are needed for the enormous quantities of evaluative and assessment information being created and for complex systems and interconnections. Highly performant knowledge-sharing infrastructure and networking would allow ready access to exemplars, to evaluations, and to the practice and views of other practitioners, rather than assume that each leadership team and learning community will devise its learning strategies anew. Research findings should be very readily available in succinct and accessible formats suitable for practitioners.

These will not only be meaningful at the micro, environment level, but will be constantly accessed and used at the meso level and at the meta level, too. The relevant sources of assessment knowledge will extend well beyond national boundaries.

Powerful knowledge systems will be cumbersome information banks unless there is the human capacity to use them fully and to interpret sensitively the information being generated. There needs to be a culture of diagnostic expertise and evaluation. This is both about the creation of professional capacity and its constant use. It is also about a democratisation of this knowledge beyond the hands of a small number of specialist experts.

Indicators of the widespread adoption of the ILE framework

After having provided an analysis of the conditions and policies that would facilitate change in the direction of the framework, we present in this section a list of indicators that would illustrate that such policies would have worked and that widespread practice of each element in the ILE 7+3 framework has been achieved. This covers both the seven learning principles and the three dimensions for innovation. Under each of the specified indicator areas, different methodologies to measure and reveal such developments might very usefully complement commonly available educational indicators.

Learning Principle One

The learning environment recognises the learners as its core participants, encourages their active engagement, and develops in them an understanding of their own activity as learners.

Cultures of schools, leadership, teachers and the local community should be actively focused on learners and learning; activity and high achievement are judged in terms of how well learners are engaged and acquire knowledge, skills and positive dispositions towards learning. The curriculum on offer should be one that young people find relevant and engaging, and one that they have had an important role in defining. Learner engagement needs to become an objective in itself. Without it, not only is the success of learning activities put in doubt, but the habits of lifelong learning are not being laid and reinforced. The need for learners to come to understand themselves as learners and become skilled in self-regulation, requires a broad professional repertoire that is at once about personalisation and about understanding the very nature of learning.

Indicators of the widespread application of Learning Principle One

Learning at the centre: Learning, learner engagement and high achievement are top priorities in the whole system and for all stakeholders, but especially for educators. This could be seen through observation and surveys of the decisions made about professional development and the organisational strategies of the different schools and learning environments.

Educators are knowledgeable and collaborative: Educators are knowledgeable about the nature of children's and young people's learning and the factors that enhance motivation and engagement. They actively participate in discussing and designing strategies collaboratively to address the needs of particular individuals and groups.

Learners' active engagement: Learners understand themselves as learners, are self-regulated and show high levels of engagement, motivation and persistence. They are prominent in goal-setting and implementation of learning activities and are an integral part of the learning leadership.

Clarity of vision: All actors involved in the learning environment are able to articulate the nature and activity of the learning taking place, as could be revealed through research or enquiry with cohorts of those actors, including importantly young people themselves.

Quality assurance: Inspection and quality assurance systems include criteria for judging learner engagement and responsibility as co-designers of learning environments.

Learning Principle Two

The learning environment is founded on the social nature of learning and actively encourages well-organised co-operative learning.

This principle militates against the fragmented models of educational organisation in which sharp boundaries exist between the work of each class and workshop, of each teacher and educator, and of each student and learner. It also is about eroding sharp boundaries between schools and communities, including the wider contacts even on a global scale. This is a prime area for continuous learning, collaboratively organised among the members of the learning community: teachers, families, learners, networks and other partners. It requires well-organised co-operative approaches that really advance learning and actively promote 21st century skills for teamwork and collaborative problem-solving.

Indicators of the widespread application of Learning Principle Two

Rich collegial activity: The nature of schools and classrooms are characterised by the "buzz" of collegial activity among and between learners and educators.

Flexible learning settings: Learning spaces, building layout, seating arrangements and the like are flexible and reflect preparedness for group work. A variety of sites for learning beyond conventional classrooms are commonplace, including different forms of community learning.

Promoting social learning: Different forms of community learning are encouraged and take place, including through the organised inter-generational contact of school-age children and seniors.

Widespread social media use: There is widespread use of social media and ICT with intense exchanges around learning projects, among and between learners and educators.

Socially rich pedagogy: Enquiry, problem-solving and project-based pedagogies are all widespread, often based on inter-disciplinarity.

Learning Principle Three

The learning professionals within the learning environment are highly attuned to the learners' motivations and the key role of emotions in achievement.

Policy debate and discourse should no longer associate emotions as "soft" and less important than the "hard" outcomes of cognitive development; promoting positive emotions and reducing negative ones are integral to learning effectiveness. This is about enhancing effectiveness, not about being "nice" towards students and making learning fun or easy. Recognition of the importance of motivation also means valuing approaches that are known to motivate young people to learn, including tech-rich applications, peer learning and non-formal community learning. Enhancing the motivation to learn – by students and teachers alike – should feature strongly in all that is being striven for by the learning leadership throughout any system.

Indicators of the widespread application of Learning Principle Three

Understanding emotions: Educators, learners and others in learning communities are articulate about and able to address learner emotions. Educational discourse will reflect the understanding of emotions and motivation as being central to learning success.

Positive challenge for every learner: Educators have deep pedagogical understanding and expertise to challenge young people without ridicule or demotivation. They use sophisticated methods to enhance sensitivity to learners' emotions and their sense of high achievement and self-efficacy. Formative assessment is widely used.

Low disengagement: Low levels of disengagement among learners can be gauged by the behaviour and attitudes of young people and, especially among those of secondary age, can be observed in the low levels of dropout and engagement among at-risk learners.

Approaches that motivate: There is a widespread use of approaches that motivate young people; this includes tech-rich learning and teaching, and non-formal, service learning in the community.

Learning Principle Four

The learning environment is acutely sensitive to the individual differences among the learners in it, including their prior knowledge.

The curriculum is devised so as to offer the choices that will meet the learning needs of all different students, and the learning environment works within these parameters to offer personalised opportunities to all. Hence curriculum policy, prior to any particular design work and sensitivity to context, should recognise that individual differences influence the success of learning and that there is "no one size fits all". A major reason for teaching and learning is precisely to alter prior knowledge. Educators, stakeholders and leadership need to become sensitive to and often expert in evaluating learning differences and in basing design decisions on such evidence.

Indicators of the widespread application of Learning Principle Four

Rich pedagogical mix: There is a large diversity and mix of pedagogical practices being exercised: shared whole-class or multi-class learning activities, targeted small group or individual learning activities for particular learners; face-to-face, virtual and blended learning; school- and community-based.

Collaborative leadership: Strong collegial work is visible through the learning leadership and with other educators and members of the learning community. This applies to system leadership as well as leadership at the level of learning environments.

Formative assessment wide and deep: There is profound formative assessment throughout learning environments, given that there is acute sensitivity to what each learner brings to the learning and to making teaching and learning effective – on any occasion and cumulatively – for each individual.

Louder learner voice: Learner agency and voice are prominent – as the learning becomes more personalised, the active role of the learners themselves becomes more powerful.

Personalised learning offers: The organisation of learning environments exhibits an important degree of flexibility regarding educational offers, use of time, and student and educator combinations so as to reflect the identified individual differences.

Learning Principle Five

The learning environment devises programmes that demand hard work and challenge from all without excessive overload.

This principle has as pre-requisite the capacity to differentiate and personalise, and is consistent with learning-centredness, engagement and motivation. Whole cultures of school systems, teachers and parents should be characterised by high expectations and avoidance of mediocrity. High expectations are crucial for effective learning, but so are the learning strategies and experiences that push and stretch all learners. Excessive overload, however, is counter-productive. Learning should not be viewed as "filling up" young people – with information, facts and knowledge – but about enhancing their understanding and their capacity to use information, facts and knowledge creatively to address new problems. Pushing learners to move beyond their comfort zones calls for instilling in them endurance and persistence in the face of adversity, which itself is much better done collectively than in isolation.

Indicators of the widespread application of Learning Principle Five

Growth mind-sets: Growth mind-sets, and not fixed ones, characterise policy and governance arrangements, just as they characterise individual learners, teachers or parents.

High expectations: There is system-wide an absence and intolerance of failure and of procedures whose main purpose is to sort and select out learners. There is an absence of dead-end programmes which receive and "park" students who have been identified as failures.

Inclusive challenge: Programmes expect hard work for each learner and pedagogies are consistent in developing talent across the whole range of achievement and interest for all students.

Personalised evidence: There is thorough-going personalisation in evidence, as educators and the wider learning communities devise ways of stretching all learners.

Learning Principle Six

The learning environment operates with clarity of expectations and deploys assessment strategies consistent with these expectations; there is strong emphasis on formative feedback to support learning.

The learning expected to be achieved and the evidence that it is being achieved need to be highly visible, in ways that are shared and understood by learners, educators and all other members of the learning community. The assessment strategies need to be consistent with and contributing to such expectations so that assessment is in the service of learning rather than inimical to it. This is true at all levels, so that learning systems as well as environments come increasingly to be formative, using extensive learning evidence at critical junctures and creating more demanding learning and teaching environments.

Indicators of the widespread application of Learning Principle Six

Clarity of expectations: There is a widespread capacity to articulate what learning expectations are by all parties in different learning environments: educators, learners, parents, and accountability and governance bodies.

Cultures of self-evaluation: Self-review and evidence-informed learning leadership become increasingly prominent aspects of learning systems.

Deep learning: There is a significant shift in influential perceptions of what constitutes acceptable assessment, away from simple pass/fail or right/wrong judgements and towards measures of deep learning, 21st century competence, engagement, foundations for lifelong learning, and so forth.

Widely shared expectations: Expectations are visible, negotiated, constructed and shared – through strong, distributed learning leadership – within learning environments and at the wider meso and meta levels. Clear, shared demanding expectations for learning are integral to equality of opportunity and a coherent teaching profession.

New assessment metrics: There are flourishing new metrics developed and in widespread use to provide learning evidence to inform decision-making. These are likely to call on new sources of expertise, and not be restricted only to the education system itself.

Learning Principle Seven

The learning environment strongly promotes "horizontal connectedness" across areas of knowledge and subjects as well as to the community and the wider world.

Connectedness, as with personalisation, assumes that strong connections are made between the world students live in and the knowledge that can enlighten and explain that world. Promoting horizontal connectedness is partly about giving learners access to the larger frameworks and knowledge structures so that individual learning episodes are made meaningful, and so that deep learning is possible. Inter-disciplinarity should be prominent. Education should find the challenging balance between connecting the learning to local experience and to families; and to going well beyond in connecting to other societies in an increasingly global world. Learning Principle Seven calls for success in both.

Indicators of the widespread application of Learning Principle Seven

Knowledge development: There is extensive evidence of work to integrate interdisciplinary knowledge around key concepts and to develop corresponding learning materials and pedagogies. There is flourishing research and development around pedagogical expertise and integrated content knowledge, not monopolised by research in universities.

Innovating assessment: New assessment metrics and qualifications are key areas for development if leaders, educators, learners, specialists, teacher educators and the diverse other stakeholders are to be incentivised to embrace greater horizontal connectedness.

Complex organisational forms: Openness to alternative solutions for making connections makes the institutional terrain more complex rather than reliance on monolithic school structures. Technology is widely adapted and used.

First dimension: Innovating the pedagogical core

The indicators that practice has shifted significantly in the direction of innovating pedagogical cores could best be developed around the four core elements – learners, educators, content and resources – and how they interact, and the four core dynamics: pedagogy, the ways in which educators work together, how learners work together and the use of time. Such indicators would be less constructed around definitions of innovation and instead seek to capture the range of different practices and models of teaching and learning that represent an intentional departure from the single-teacher/whole-class model, frontal teaching pedagogies, and the standard lesson time unit. Innovating the pedagogical core implies the presence of diverse educators, the use of technology, the application of curricula focused on 21st century skills, sustainability and inter-disciplinarity.

Indicators of the widespread practice of innovating pedagogical cores

Expanding learner profiles: Learning environments bring together learners who would otherwise be separated (remotely distant, different ages), include others as learners (senior adults, parents) and reach non-traditional learners (the disengaged and those risking dropout, those with special needs, etc.).

Diverse educator profiles: The profile of teacher expands to include others. An important number of educators, experts and volunteers beyond the conventional teaching force is involved in the schooling (parents, peers, university researchers, community and business experts, etc.).

Innovating content: Project-based, inquiry work aiming to develop 21st century skills is common practice. There is extensive work on integrating interdisciplinary knowledge around key concepts and developing corresponding learning materials and pedagogies. There is flourishing research and development around specialist pedagogical expertise as well as integrated content knowledge.

Innovating resource use: There is widespread use of social media and ICT. Learners engage in research and intense exchanges around learning projects. Teaching, learning and pedagogy are often tech-rich. Learning takes place at all times and in a variety of physical and virtual sites, and there is wide use of community facilities (museums, libraries, theatres, sports centres, community centres and the like) for teaching and learning.

Innovating pedagogy: System-wide there is a rich mix and diversity of pedagogical practices, including whole-class, small group and individual study; direct contact, virtual and blended learning; school- and community-based. Personalised approaches and formative assessment are highly visible, as are active pedagogies.

Strong relations and collaboration: Educators constantly connect with each other, with learners, and with other partners and networks, especially through technology-rich learning communities.

Flexible use of time: An important proportion of learning time is spent in groups of different sizes, taught by more than one educator; in online learning and in non-formal learning, in and out of the school. More flexible use of learning time ensures personalised timetables and allows for deep learning.

Second dimension: Learning leadership and the formative cycle

Leadership is critical for reform and innovation at all levels of the system. Its core business is to create and sustain environments that are conducive to effective learning. It is exercised through strong visions and corresponding strategies intensely focused on learning via shared, collaborative activity. Teacher engagement and professional learning are key aspects of the design and implementation process. The learners themselves should be privileged and influential players. Just as formative feedback should be integral to individual classes, so should it permeate the organisation as a whole so that it operates formatively – information-rich about the learning taking place, to be constantly fed back to the different stakeholders and into revised strategies for learning and further innovation. This means strong processes of self-evaluation and the constant endeavour of sharing knowledge about learning.

Indicators of the widespread practice of the learning leadership and formative cycle

Learning as the core business: The leadership at different levels of the system places learning at the heart of decision-making and strategies.

Extending leadership profiles: There is a strong focus on learning and design, and decision making is distributed and shared, bringing in the professional community, learners and other stakeholders, including foundations.

Information-rich systems: Information systems are sophisticated and highly developed. Individual portfolios are well developed and widely used, making the learning history, wide capabilities and achievements of each learner accessible to all engaged in designing the teaching, strategy and the learning environment.

Using learning evidence and evaluation: There is a dominant culture and practice of evaluative thinking and self-review and of using evaluative evidence formatively to inform design strategies, with significant amounts of time devoted to it. The learning community shows demonstrable knowledge of the state of learning within it at any one time and how this has changed over recent time.

New evaluation and assessment metrics: There are flourishing new metrics developed and in widespread use. These reflect the aims of learning environments and wider system metrics, and include mastery, understanding, capacity to transfer and use knowledge, curiosity, creativity, teamwork and persistence. Assessment extends outside conventional school settings. Quality assurance systems, including inspection, recognise successful learner engagement and exercise of voice.

Enhanced meso-level arrangements: Widespread connected leadership arrangements are in place across districts, networks, chains and communities of practice, whether formed spontaneously or through formalised strategies and networks.

Third dimension: Partnerships to extend capacity and horizons

The contemporary learning environment needs to develop strong connections with partners so as to extend its boundaries, resources and learning spaces. Such extensions should include: parents and families as active partners, stakeholders and actors in the educational process; local community bodies, businesses, and cultural institutions; higher education; and other schools and learning environments through networks. Communication technologies and social media represent powerful means for these partnerships to flourish, offering platforms for parents, learners and teachers to communicate, collaborate, share and access information. Creating wider partnerships helps overcome the limitations of isolation in order to acquire the expertise, knowledge partners and synergies. This also relates to learning principle seven – "promoting horizontal connectedness" – within the educational world and beyond it.

Indicators of the widespread practice of partnerships

High visibility of partners: Partners are actively involved in the learning environment. They are visible in the teaching and learning, professional development, evaluation and leadership. Partners are in direct contact with learners and are an integral part of the pedagogical core and formative learning leadership rather than external to it and providing only sponsorship and support.

Density of meso-level activity: Extended collaboration with partners, including other learning environments, means the highly visible measurable existence of the meso level across districts, networks, chains, and communities of practice, whether formed spontaneously or through formalised strategies and networking initiatives.

Global connection: In a global world, it is common practice that partnership contacts, with other learning environments and different stakeholders, extend beyond national boundaries.

Main summary highlights

For the ILE framework to have generalised impact, it must be fostered well beyond individual schools and learning communities. This chapter has addressed two main questions: first, what kinds of broader changes and conditions are needed to help these overall design principles to become commonplace features of learning systems? Second, what will we expect to see as revealing indicators that the framework and its features have become widespread?

Conducive conditions and policies for promoting the ILE framework are summarised under the following headings:

- reducing standardisation, fostering innovation, broadening institutions
- appropriate accountability and metrics for 21st century learning

- fostering learning leadership, trust and learner agency
- widespread collaborative expert professionalism
- ubiquitous professional learning
- connectivity and extensive digital infrastructure
- flourishing cultures of networks and partnership
- powerful knowledge systems and cultures of evaluation.

Many of the indicators that reveal one of the elements in the 7+3 framework reveals others too. A condensed set offers more summary areas where measures could be developed to show whether societies are making strides to put the framework into common practice. It would be helpful for systems to compare existing statistics and indicators with this set and to address the methodological challenges of developing precise measures in each.

- *High learning activity and motivation levels:* There will be measurably high levels of engagement and persistence by learners. The nature of schools and classrooms is characterised by the "buzz" of collegial activity and learning. The extent to which young people spend time in a variety of sites for learning beyond conventional classrooms can be demonstrated, including different forms of community learning.
- *Prominent learner agency and voice:* As the learning becomes more personalised, the active role of the learners becomes more evident. Learners are active in learning leadership teams right across systems.
- *Educators actively discuss learning strategies and practice collaboration:* The indicators reveal how readily teachers and other educators engage in professional discussion about learning strategies in general and in relation to individual learners. Indicators of teacher practice show readiness to engage with learning leadership, innovation and professional collaboration, including team teaching.
- *Educators are highly knowledgeable about learning:* Indicators of teacher knowledge show widespread familiarity with the ILE Learning Principles as well as with a rich repertoire of teaching strategies for putting them into practice.
- *Mixed, personalised pedagogical practices:* System-wide there is a rich mix and diversity of pedagogical practices. Personalised approaches and formative assessment are highly visible, as are active pedagogies.
- *Inter-disciplinarity, curriculum development and new learning materials:* there will have been extensive work to integrate knowledge, materials and pedagogies around key concepts and learning matter. There is flourishing research and development (R&D) around pedagogical expertise and integrated content knowledge, shared across system boundaries and extending well beyond university research.
- *Widespread innovative applications of digital resources and social media:* There is widespread use of social media and ICT as learners engage in research and intense exchanges around learning projects and educators connect with each other, with learners, and with other partners and networks. Teaching, learning and pedagogy are typically (though not always) tech-rich.
- *Cultures of using learning evidence and evaluation:* There is a dominant culture and practice of evaluative thinking and self-review and of using evaluative evidence formatively to inform design strategies. Significant amounts of time are devoted to it and knowledge is widespread

among learning environment participants of the state of learning within it, at any one time and recent changes.

- *Sophisticated information systems and individual portfolios* are highly developed and widely available; detailed learner profiles and learning histories are readily accessible with appropriate privacy safeguards for those designing teaching, strategy and the learning environment.
- *New evaluation and assessment metrics:* There are flourishing new metrics in widespread application. These reflect the aims of learning environments as well as the wider system metrics around what are commonly termed 21st century competences. Assessment extends well outside conventional school settings and quality assurance recognises learner engagement and the exercise of voice.
- *Diverse partners highly visible:* Indicators would reveal the diversity of partners who are now commonly active in pedagogical cores and learning leadership, with decision making typically shared and bringing in the professional community, learners and other stakeholders, including foundations.
- *A thriving, vibrant meso level:* High levels of collaboration and engagement with partners, including other learning environments, mean the visible and tangible emergence of a strong meso level, formal and non-formal, across districts, networks, chains, and communities of practice.
- *Dense global connections:* In a global world, it is common practice that partnerships and contacts with other learning environments and different stakeholders extend beyond system boundaries.

References

Cerna, L. (2014), "Trust: What it is and why it matters for governance and education", *OECD Education Working Papers*, No. 108, OECD Publishing, Paris, http://dx.doi.org/10.1787/5jxswcg0t6wl-en.

Dumont, H., D. Istance and F. Benavides (eds.) (2010), *The Nature of Learning: Using Research to Inspire Practice*, Educational Research and Innovation, OECD Publishing, Paris, http://dx.doi.org/10.1787/9789264086487-en.

OECD (2013), *Innovative Learning Environments*, Educational Research and Innovation, OECD Publishing, Paris, http://dx.doi.org/10.1787/9789264203488-en.

Chapter 3

Promising strategies for spreading innovative learning environments

This chapter provides an overview of the strategies and initiatives that were contributed to the "Implementation and Change" strand of the ILE study. Altogether, 26 participating systems, including countries, provincial states, foundations and networks, submitted promising examples of change strategies. Each is described briefly in turn. The chapter then identifies underlying threads summarised as a series of C's: Culture change, which is more important but much harder to realise than surface change; Clarifying focus, as trying to do all at once risks disjointed diffusion and dilution; Capacity creation, consisting of knowledge (including research), professional learning and the capacity to act on that knowledge and learning; Collaboration and co-operation, for collaborative professionalism is assumed in many strategies as are networks and professional learning communities; Communication technologies and platforms as prominent parts of professional practice and change strategies; and Change agents, i.e. specific specialist roles providing local drive, expertise and influence.

The next three chapters turn to the strategies and initiatives submitted to the ILE project, with this particular chapter offering an overview and identifying some common themes and threads running through them. Those submitted represent, of course, only a tiny number of the possible initiatives and strategies around the world that might have been considered. They are the ones selected by the systems which engaged actively in the OECD/ILE work and who thus had the knowledge and means, as well as the desire, to take part in this international study. The featured strategies and initiatives can make no claim to special effectiveness; in any case, it is questionable whether any strategy can make the bold claim to be "global best practice" when so much depends on the context and the unique social and political circumstances in each setting. Instead, they provide a fascinating set of cases from which to gain insights into the range of approaches being taken to spread and sustain innovative learning in different systems around the world.

The chapter identifies a set of underlying threads that run through the diverse strategies and initiatives, which are summarised as a series of C's: creation, context, complexity, communication, communities, collaboration, capacities, conditions and climates (an initial summary of these features appeared in the first edition of a new OECD education policy flagship [OECD, 2015]). They do not add up to recipes of success but highlight some of the promising strategies and initiatives being tried in different countries. On this basis, the following two chapters analyse more closely the nature of innovation, implementation and change in 21st century learning systems, first (Chapter 4) at the meso level and then (Chapter 5) at the wider meta level.

Gathering promising strategies and initiatives for the international study

In inviting systems to join this strand of the ILE study we were inviting them to share examples through common protocols of promising ways for spreading and sustaining innovative learning. Whereas the "innovative cases" ILE strand had looked at particular learning environments, in this final strand, the horizon was broadened from individual examples towards change strategies that necessarily involve several, even many, different sites. We emphasised that such examples needed to have operated through time so giving evidence of implementation, rather than initiatives that were still at the planning and promise stage.

Consistent with the rest of the ILE project, the focus was on learning arrangements for children and young people, understood broadly as referring to 3-19 year-olds or age bands within (see Dumont, Istance and Benavides, 2010; OECD 2013a; OECD, 2013b). They might cover a variety of different approaches, often in combination: direct promotion of innovation, the provision of incentives, network creation, knowledge management, leadership strategies and other professional development capacity building, creating new forms of expertise and change management, and more general drives to create climates favourable for innovative learning. They could target change in one or more of the different components of learning environments: particular learner groups; the learning professionals; content; materials, facilities, and technologies; and the different ways in which these are organised and assessed. We made clear that we were not looking for general reforms of the curriculum, institutional structures, and the management or governance of schooling that did not have the intention first and foremost to innovate learning environments.

The aim in compiling these strategies and initiatives was to learn from the experiences and approaches taken, and to use these examples to inform the wider frameworks being constructed by the ILE study. Creating frameworks has been a guiding objective of the ILE study, frameworks that we hope will last much longer than the details of specific initiatives that are constantly changing (several of which may have disappeared by the time this report goes into print). But the aim was also to get closer to the strategies and systems themselves and to work directly with them. Thus, the study has been research and development (R&D) rather than pure research, and indeed it might be more appropriate to think of it as development and research (D&R) with practice leading the research, rather than the other way round (Bentley and Gillinson, 2007).

The strategies and initiatives submitted to ILE

Australia (South Australia): The South Australian Department for Education and Child Development (DECD) has sought to build innovation momentum. Strategies have included conferences, establishing a website and newsletters to share innovative practices, undertaking research and creating a community of practice from the most innovative schools. A Research and Innovation Framework was developed by late 2011 and innovation became part of the Department's strategic plan. The focus has been on equity, excellence and sustainability, identifying and up-scaling innovation, as well as establishing system-wide directions for innovation.

Australia (Victoria): Reform in the Western Metropolitan Region was a systemic intervention strategy, designed to galvanise a collective effort to lift performance. The focus was primarily on improvement in literacy and numeracy initially, subsequently extended to other areas of the curriculum. System-wide improvement was generated through a process of co-design and mutual commitment between the region and all schools.

Austria: The rationale for the school reform "New Secondary School" (NMS) is that reform must happen in schools to be effective yet must be widely implemented to be systemic. It works through change agents and these need to be networked and to operate as communities of practice. NMS began in 2008 in 67 pilot schools and has since led to a mandated school reform, to be phased in completely by 2018. It aims to foster innovative learning environments and equity. Each NMS designates a member of the teaching staff to be the Lerndesigner, which is a very significant system intervention in a country in which schools have flat hierarchies with the predominance up until now of the autonomy-parity pattern.

Belgium (French community): The aim of Décolâge!, with 300 schools engaged in April 2014 and about half (75) the psycho-medico-social centres in the system, has been to reduce grade repetition in the very early years of schooling and for this to be the strategic focus for consolidating a much wider set of changes related to pedagogical practice and under-achievement. It assumes that this requires innovation and credible alternative practice, which in turn means reaching and mobilising all the professionals and other adults involved in the identification and implementation of such alternatives.

Canada (Alberta): The Canadian Rockies Public Schools District worked with OECD/ILE in hosting an international conference in 2011 in Banff, and in promoting its initiative "Inspiring Hearts and Minds". The initiative was centred around consultation to identify community values, education trends and major forces of change. It is grounded on making connections and breaking down artificial boundaries and two overarching emergent themes are: i) the whole child (intellectual, emotional, social, physical and spiritual development); and ii) schools as the centre of learning and development in the community.

Canada (British Columbia): The featured initiatives are three school-to-school networks – the Network of Performance Based Schools (NPBS), the Aboriginal Enhancement Schools Network (AESN), and the Healthy Schools Network (HSN) – that operate in tandem with a graduate programme to promote learning leadership and innovation (Certificate in Innovative Educational Leadership). The learning leadership development is deeply rooted in cycles of inquiry, and prominently uses the ILE Learning Principles.

Chile: Chile's initiatives are a series of programmes and awards in the service of innovating learning. The programmes cover: the Enlaces Programme; the Programme for Innovative Teaching for Deeper Learning; the UAI Centre for innovation and learning; and diverse strands of the Chile Foundation. The networks include: the Network of Innovative Teachers; the regional network Innovemos; the Microsoft Alliance for Education; and the Network for Leading Schools. Among the awards are: the Telefonica Foundation Award for Educational Innovation; the Ibero-American award to Educational Innovation; and the competition "I innovate in class, integrating technologies".

Finland: "Schools on the Move" is a national action strategy aiming to establish a physically active culture in comprehensive schools. After piloting from 2010 to 2012, it has grown nationwide, supported by new data and analysis on the relationship between physical activity and children's learning and well-being.

Former Yugoslav Republic of Macedonia (UNICEF): The in-service Teacher Education Programme on Early Numeracy and Literacy is addressing low achievement. It is building capacity from the bottom up to stimulate long-term system change by changing teacher practice. At the same time, it is about changing from the top through a different professional development model, training all teachers in the new programme, and equipping advisors to support these developments. It was implemented in teacher training and began modelling teacher professional development and support from 2009 onwards.

France: The aim of RESPIRE is to create a platform for educators to share their knowledge, practice, problems and resources, and to strengthen professionalism. It combines design and management by the Education Ministry's department of R&D with technological support by a regional education knowledge centre. It includes a continuously updated knowledge bank of innovations (more than 2 500 innovations already compiled and updated) and supports communities of practice and professional learning communities. It facilitates the mediation of knowledge between practitioners through sharing knowledge and experiences, experiments and initiatives, projects and best practices.

Germany (Baden-Württemberg): The Gemeinschaftsschule is a new type of school within the formal system: 42 such schools started in 2012/2013, with another 87 following in 2013/2014. Its principles include: strong emphasis on equity and on co-operative learning; teachers seeing themselves as specialists in their respective fields, as experts at diagnosing students' needs, skills and knowledge, and as learning facilitators; providing an all-day structured space for learning. This concept of schooling is a departure from earlier models and is recognised as having far-reaching implications for the curriculum and teacher education.

Germany (Thuringia): "Development of Inclusive and Innovative Learning Environments" is an initiative of the Thuringian Ministry for Education, Science and Culture (TMBWK) within the framework of the strategy "Education for Sustainable Development". A key concept is "Gestaltungskompetenz", or competence to shape the future: foresight thinking, interdisciplinary knowledge, independent action and participation in societal decision making. It is working through approximately 40 "reference" or exemplary schools.

Israel: The Ministry of Education's Experiments and Entrepreneurship Division identifies schools and educators with a robust vision, and engages them in a five-year innovation support process. This includes analysis and evaluation, and the provision of support, training and R&D tools. As time progresses, the ministry requires the innovation to be applied with ever-increasing scope, and at the end of the period the initiative or school completes an experiment book. Those demonstrating special success become dissemination centres for others interested in developing similar innovations.

Korea: Strategies of organisation and systems focused on multicultural education have prominently included the establishment of the Centre for Multicultural Education as a special institution supported by the Ministry of Education, Science and Technology in order to lead research into multicultural policies and innovative implementation. This has been complemented by the establishment of the Hanul Club as a target school carrying out innovative multicultural education, planned and supported by Provincial Educational Office, including the innovative Rainbow Chorus.

Mexico (Conafe): The featured strategy is about organising interventions with teaching professionals called Itinerant Pedagogical Advisors (APIs), to improve learning for children in rural and disadvantaged communities. The APIs work collaboratively with the Leaders for Community Education, who are young students from high school giving educational social service. The APIs thereby strengthen teaching and learning, all with the active participation and collaboration of parents. The API is co-ordinated centrally by the organisation Conafe and operated by delegations in each of the states in Mexico.

Mexico (UNETE): UNETE, the Association of Business People in Educational Technology, is a non-profit organisation supporting educational quality and equity in Mexico. In 2009, UNETE began pilots in 128 schools in 15 states. These aimed to deepen understanding of the integration of ICT into teaching and learning; identify the impact on academic performance of ICT integration; scale up the training for and monitoring of technology practices; identify best practice innovations using ICT; and analyse the impact of implementing specific pilot programs in different schools. The pilots themselves are completed though evaluation is continuing.

New Zealand: "Learning and Change Networks" is a government-initiated strategy to establish a web of knowledge-sharing networks among schools and kura kaupapa Māori (Māori immersion schools), families/whānau, teachers, leaders, communities, professional providers and the Ministry of Education. The network participants work collaboratively to accelerate student achievement in years 1 to 8 and address the equity challenge. Participants in networks work through four development phases: (i) establishing infrastructure to operate as a network across schools and communities; (ii) profiling the current learning environments to understand strengths, supports and challenges and agree on change priorities; (iii) implementing a plan to address the change priorities; and (iv) sustaining valuable change and agreeing on next steps for building the future.

Norway: The National Advisory Team programme assists those who run schools including principals to improve their leadership and learning environments. A team of advisors has been established at a national level to support schools with quality challenges in areas such as students lacking in reading and mathematics skills, under-performing learning environments, and students and apprentices who do not complete or are not passing higher schools exams.

Peru (Innova Schools): This is a network of 22 schools (2014), aiming to reach 70 by 2020. The aim is to offer an alternative that is excellent, scalable and affordable. It is implementing what in its context is a paradigm shift: from teacher-centred to student-centred teaching and learning models, with innovative pedagogies and time use. Technology is regarded as an important tool in the learning process. It uses a blended learning model and an innovation programme that invites students to tackle issues in their community, connecting what they learn in the classroom to the real world, in a framework of open-ended learning.

Peru (Lego Education): This foundation is joining with the Education Ministry to stimulate and motivate students and promote teacher learning communities. The programme includes the provision of 130 000 Education WeDo robotics kits, 30 000 teacher guides with technical content aimed at guiding elementary school teachers, and training of 50 specialists of the Ministry of Education, face-to-face training for 8 000 teachers conducted in 24 regions of Peru, and virtual training via the Internet for 7 000 teachers.

Slovenia: The featured policy initiative is designed to spread and sustain innovative learning in Slovenian schools, based on the principles of empowerment and shared leadership. It combines direct promotion, provision of incentives, network creation, knowledge management, leadership strategies and other professional development capacity building, creating new forms of expertise and change management, and more general drives to create climates favourable to innovative learning. Initial work in ten schools then spread to all gymnasia, and now it is being extended to primary schools. The whole process has lasted over ten years.

South Africa (KwaZulu-Natal): The ICT in Education (ICT-Ed) project aims to address the quality of teaching and learning in the classroom by replacing traditional teacher-centred teaching with a learner-centred technology-based teaching and learning programme. Several of these schools will also receive a school-strengthening programme that addresses barriers to learning and development.

Spain: "Curricular Integration of Key Competences" is an initiative of the Ministry of Education, Culture and Sport together with the Autonomous Communities. It aims to improve key competences development and is being implemented through the National Centre for Educational Innovation and Research. In the first stage, 150 primary and secondary schools, both public and state-supported, were selected in two categories of preparedness. "Initiating Schools" are for the teachers to reflect on their own practice and to get initiated into the competence-based syllabus; in "Advanced Schools", the aim is to build a common view shared by each teaching team.

Sweden: Mother Tongue Theme is an innovative platform to build, maintain and inspire networks of mother tongue teachers and school leaders. A key part of this is the Mother Tongue Theme website which serves as a knowledge platform for mother tongue teachers in Sweden, Norway and beyond. In 2003, it was awarded the Best Global Website Award for "the most innovative multilingual and multicultural site in Europe". Now, 100 teachers and school leaders contribute to the site with unique content in 45 different languages.

Switzerland (Ticino): The School Improvement Advisor (SIA) initiative aims to help schools and teachers to develop innovative teaching methodologies and to practise self-evaluation. The action of the SIA as coach, critical friend and professional in educational investigation is to help put innovation into practice. The targeted learners are young apprentices and students in the Swiss vocational sector in schools mainly in the industrial and commercial fields.

United Kingdom (England): Whole Education is a partnership network of schools, organisations and individuals that believe that all young people should have a fully rounded education, developing the knowledge, skills and qualities needed to help them thrive in life and work. It is supporting the spread of innovative practice and change across a self-elected, bottom-up community of practice of schools. It has lead Partner Schools, Pathfinder Schools and then a larger group of less active Network Schools across the country (mainly England), all supporting and learning from each other.

Hence, the strategies covered vary widely. Several are directly led and organised by the national ministry of education but in others the ministry has more of a support role or else the initiative is not happening at the national level or it is being led from elsewhere altogether, such as by foundations. In some it is about building capacity, in others it is about establishing the platforms for a range of stakeholders to build their own capacity and share practice and knowledge. Some are based on digital technology while others address particular groups of learners or have a specific content focus such as well-being or futures competence. Some only cover a relatively small network of schools while others have gone or will go system-wide, with many between the extremes.

Emerging threads in innovation learning strategies – the C's

There has thus been a wide range of approaches gathered by the ILE study. Despite widely differing contexts, there are some common themes shared by them. We do not pretend that there is a single set of shared features of "best practice" to be distilled from these examples. The appropriateness of strategies depends critically on context; some initiatives are more ambitious or radical than others, and different approaches are apparent. The purpose here is to capture certain key features amid all the programme detail.

Culture change

Several of the strategies emphasise the importance of creating culture change in schools as more important than surface change but also much more difficult to realise. The Victorian WMR reform in Australia, for instance, took as its ambition to change the "mind-set" of schools to aspire to major improvement, changing the instructional practices of the school leaders and teachers and the system providing intense and step-by-step support. The system-wide renovation in Slovenia began from the understanding that past reforms had been excessively top-down so that there was insufficient ownership of them by the local actors who matter. The need for new kinds of knowledge and new kinds of schools as learning communities amounted to a veritable culture change, in particular in accepting the importance of being more collaborative and connected. In this case, training in moderation skills was needed given the lack of experience with collaboration. The KwaZulu-Natal initiative in South Africa like the Innova Schools Network in Peru were clear that this calls for a culture change to move to more active modes of teaching and learning from traditional methods that fail far too many students.

Clarifying focus

Many of the innovation strategies reported to OECD/ILE are aimed right at such mainstream goals as addressing low educational achievement and enhancing quality. Innovation is necessary because repeating variants of conventional approaches have failed to dent such stubborn and persistent problems as continued low achievement among the same groups of students. In some cases, innovating learning environments is seen not just as a means to these widely shared equity and quality goals, but as an end in itself. Strengthening the focus on learning is also an explicit goal of several, making schools more learning-centred and getting students to accomplish deep learning rather than superficial mastery. Some have a strong future focus: both Thuringia and Spain, for example, are working to spread new content around 21st century skills and futures literacy.

Several of the systems emphasise the importance of clear focus whatever the specific objectives, rejecting the notion of "letting 1 000 flowers bloom". Both British Columbia and New Zealand report a relentless recourse to learning evidence to ensure that network innovation activity is disciplined and focused, encouraging accountability and knowledge sharing. Trying to cover everything all at once risks disjointed diffusion of effort and missing all targets in the process. Several systems report how choices needed to be made to ensure focus while avoiding narrow goal-setting that blinkers wider innovation. Many networks, for instance, choose improving writing as a core focus for attention in improvement but see it as the vehicle through which wider innovations can be built. Similarly, the French Belgian initiative Décolâge! has been strongly focused on reducing grade repetition in the very early years of schooling as the strategic means for consolidating a much wider set of changes related to classroom practice and under-achievement.

Capacity creation and collaboration

Knowledge creation and mediation are central features of many of the strategies to innovate learning environments, and to grow and sustain them. This has been a long standing focus of OECD/CERI analysis (e.g. OECD, 2004; OECD, 2009). Many different ways are used to share knowledge and to capture the learning that is continually taking place through the innovation.

Several of the strategies place as a cornerstone of the reform drive the need to generate knowledge about the student learning that is taking place, and for that knowledge to be acted upon. The New Zealand Learning and Change Networks strategy has participants engage at the outset in deep learning for up to six months: profiling the current learning environment to understand student achievement challenges and agree on change priorities, as well as on the learning, teaching, leadership and family support practices that are useful and those that should be changed. In Victoria, the Western Metropolitan Region strategy has been designed around rigorous performance analysis, a unified leadership focused on building commitment and capacity, training and practice in evidence-based classroom techniques, and the provision of additional resources and support.

Box 3.1. **Slovenia: Renovation through school development teams**

The general aim has been to gain two sustainable effects:

1. to stimulate didactic innovations by individual teachers and interdisciplinary teams in order to develop higher-order thinking and competences
2. to introduce and sustain such change through strategic planning and reflective implementation and co-ordination across whole schools.

At the beginning, the main focus was on the first of these two aims but this has tended to shift to the second.

The reform combines different approaches and instruments, such as direct promotion, provision of incentives, network creation, knowledge management, leadership strategies and other professional development capacity building, creating new forms of expertise and change management, and the more general drive to create climates favourable to innovative learning. It involves different groups and elements: learning professionals; the students; concepts of change management, learning and teaching, and knowledge; materials, facilities and technologies to be organised and combined in many different ways. It developed an institute of change agents, research and professional development network programmes, and networking.

The whole process has lasted for around ten years but its main features were designed and implemented in the first three years. Ten schools were part of this initial pilot phase, but it then spread to all gymnasia (over 70 schools), and it is now being extended to primary schools. Over time, more and more activities have been put in the hands of schools themselves for when people are not included they do not feel the changes and innovations as their own. The most important transforming idea was that of co-design with teachers in which they come to take lead responsibility drawing on national materials and support.

Source: Slovenia Notes, http://www.oecd.org/edu/ceri/implementationandchange.htm.

A research component is often critical both to understand how the strategy is working and to create the materials on which it can be further strengthened and sustained through such means as teacher education and leadership development. For instance, research and observation have been "drivers of change" in the Catalonia/Jaume Bofill Foundation strategy to promote innovative learning leadership (Jolonch, Martinez and Badia, 2013). Such research very usefully informs an understanding of implementation, not just what works in ideal conditions. Those schools and projects that participate in innovation programmes with additional funding may be required as a condition of their participation to write up their approaches and materials into handbooks to be shared with others, as in the "experimental" schools chosen by the Experiments and Entrepreneurship Division of the Israeli Ministry of Education.

The South Australia evaluation of their ILE strategy pointed to the value of the practitioner action research within the Innovation Community of Practice. The identified longer-term impacts included the value of literature and research as the basis for discussions about innovative practice, the validation of innovative practices, and in general for enhanced understanding and better design.

So important is the creation of expert knowledge and converting that into accessible forms and formats that it may call for specialist institutes for this purpose as an integral part of the reform strategy. In the case of the Austrian NMS Reform this was achieved through the creation of the National Centre for Learning Schools (CLS). Its primary objectives are to:

- sustain and foster school networks and communities of practice
- develop change agents through qualification programmes, symposia and networking
- integrate findings from current learning research into the NMS environment to development strategies
- disseminate next practice insights and examples on line and in print
- support change processes in teacher education to meet the goals of the NMS

- exploit system-wide synergy potentials
- provide support for policy and programme development.

Extensive evaluation is integral to the Austrian reform, mixing large national quantitative and smaller qualitative research, and incorporating the results into the qualification programme and into specially-developed protocols for evaluation. Similarly, in Slovenia, the National Education Institute has been crucial to the reform – in partnership with the ministry and the consortia of gymnasia. In South Australia, the innovations are linked to a local university where honours students provide research to feed back into the innovation process.

Professional learning goes hand-in-hand with knowledge in strategies to spread innovative learning environments. The CIEL programme in British Columbia immerses participants in research knowledge about leadership and learning with a view to providing them with deep understanding and knowledge appropriate for context with a strong focus on inquiry. The creation of the *Lerndesigner* change agents as part of the NMS Reform in Austria involved equally the organisation of *lernateliers* where these new actors in educational innovation come together for professional learning and exchange. There is a specific *Lerndesigner* qualification jointly organised by the national centre (responsible for national *lernateliers*) and the university colleges of teacher education (*Pedagogic Hochschule*, responsible for the regional *lernateliers*). It takes two years to reskill and newly-skill *Lerndesigners* in mindfulness of learning, difference and diversity, competence orientation, "backwards design" curriculum development, differentiated instruction, and assessment. The recognition and expertise that comes with such deep learning has strengthened the reform effort throughout.

Box 3.2. **UNICEF: Teacher Education programme (Former Yugoslav Republic of Macedonia)**

In the Former Yugoslav Republic of Macedonia, the Bureau for Education Development (BED) with the support of UNICEF has developed and implemented the Teacher Education Programme on Early Numeracy and Literacy. This programme started in 2009 and aims at training, mentoring and changing teachers' practice in order to improve learning outcomes in the targeted areas. In 2009, the programme started in 34 primary schools; by the 2014-2015 school year, all (350) primary schools of the country participated in the numeracy programme and almost half of them (149) participated in the literacy one.

The initiative includes a "training the trainer" strategy. BED advisors work with professional communities of teachers called Regional Learning Teams (RLT), providing their participants with new knowledge and skills for their teaching practice. They also train them in how to transfer knowledge to other teachers and how to support them. Members of the RLTs then act as guides to their peers in their own schools observing and monitoring their work using "fidelity tools", gathering data, providing formative feedback to teachers and helping them improve their practice through the use of innovative learning methods and techniques.

During the programme, each school is visited at least three times in the course of one school year to assess progress in implementing the programme, the achievements and the challenges that the teachers and the schools are faced with, and to provide schools and teachers with professional support.

Based on the experience with implementation, in 2014 the Ministry of Education and Science (MoES) and BDE revised the curriculum in mathematics for the first cycle of primary education with the support of the Cambridge International Examination Centre Programme. It has now been officially introduced into all primary schools.

Highly positive outcomes of this initiative have been registered as teachers not only have improved the quality of their practice but also are more confident and satisfied. More collaboration within and beyond schools and more involvement of teachers becoming mentors of other teachers have also been noticed. Learners have improved both in numeracy and reading, and are more confident and actively engaged in their own learning. The physical learning environments have also been used more creatively, and head teachers have become more supportive of innovation. As for the model, it has proved to be effective as well as replicable, and it can be applied to other regions and to other initiatives in the education sector.

Source: UNICEF (Former Yugoslav Republic of Macedonia) Notes, http://www.oecd.org/edu/ceri/implementationandchange.htm.

Organisational routines that have at their core the aim of keeping learning at the centre of all school activity are very promising when they change the organisational cultures of teachers and schools through collaboration, observation and feedback, and professional learning. Such routines include approaches like Lesson Study and Learning Study associated particularly with Japan and Hong Kong as summarised in Cheng and Mo (2013). They also include the "kernel routines" discussed in an earlier ILE volume (Resnick et al., 2010), summarised thus:

> When chosen purposefully and implemented well, new organisational routines can function as powerful instruments for transforming school practice[...] Rather than attempting to drive out current practices, the kernel routine recruits and "re-purposes" the familiar ways of doing things[...] [with] clear articulation of the steps in the routine, the rationale for these steps, and the requirements of each one. This calls for training procedures and a set of tools and artefacts for performing the routine (p. 293).

The Victorian WMR School Improvement at Scale strategy also used observational and collaborative "learning walk" routines for professional learning and culture change. Policy strategies to promote such organisational routines revolve around promoting professional learning in these different methods and approaches and facilitating communities of practice that are actively applying them.

Networks and professional learning communities are thus a widespread feature of strategies for growing and sustaining innovative learning. By their nature, they are based on voluntary and motivated engagement rather than obligation: while this may seem ephemeral compared with the solidity of well-defined educational structures, this is becoming the natural form of collective action in contemporary learning systems.

Box 3.3. **New Zealand: The Learning and Change Network Strategy**

The Learning and Change Network Strategy seeks to learn from a period of widespread experimentation to bring together schools and kura, communities, professional providers and the Ministry of Education to work collaboratively to accelerate student achievement in years 1 to 8. Learning and Change Networks are addressing three big agenda items - schooling improvement, blended learning and digital technologies, and cultural responsiveness - holistically instead of creating projects that deal with those agendas separately.

Design work on the strategy commenced in October 2011 and five pilot networks representing 55 schools/ kura were established. The strategy went live in October 2012 with 57 networks established involving 373 schools/kura (approximately 15% of New Zealand schools/kura), with an average of 6 to 7 schools per network. There is a particular focus on priority groups traditionally under-served by the system – Māori, Pasifika, those from lower socio-economic groups, and those with special education needs – along with their families/ whānau, teachers, school and community leaders.

Among its distinctive features are:

- *a tight and highly-developed methodology* for ensuring a strong focus on learning and learning change, including very explicit tools, procedures, support, and facilitation
- an explicit and prominent focus on *engaging learners, their parents, families/whānau and communities* in powerful learning-focused partnerships because they are strategic stakeholders in achieving learning outcomes
- a developed applied theory of *making professional learning communities and networks work* so as to achieve outcomes that individual schools and teachers cannot readily do by themselves
- a *sophisticated set of leadership and management arrangements* that puts the onus for action and change on the networks and their members, while embedding these in regional and national structures of support
- a central role is given to *evaluation*, generating learning evidence at school, network, regional and system levels
- a strong connection to international experience and networks.

Source: New Zealand Notes, http://www.oecd.org/edu/ceri/implementationandchange.htm.

While networking depends on voluntary and motivated professional engagement among local professionals and stakeholders, there is still a clear policy role in helping to establish the climate and means for effective networking. One obvious way in which this can be done is to support the establishment of online platforms for teacher learning and networking, as discussed next.

Communication technologies and platforms

Technology contributes to all the different components, relationships, partnerships and principles that are integral to innovative learning environments, whether through innovating the pedagogical core, facilitating the learning leadership and formative organisation cycle, or through extending capacity in rich networks of partnership. There is not a single "technology effect" rooted in pedagogical practice but ICT can and should permeate in a myriad ways throughout learning environments and systems (Istance and Kools, 2013). In the 21st century it is obvious that digital communication should be prominent in any strategy for growing and sustaining innovative learning environments at scale, that seeks to overcome the limits of time, place and resources in order to share knowledge and to build communities of practice at scale.

Box 3.4. **France: Learning and innovative professional communities in the social network RESPIRE**

The aim of the website is to create the best conditions for educators to share their knowledge and practice, their problems and resources, and to strengthen their professionalism. It enhances also collegiality and solidarity between distant schools at national level. Three factors gave life to the process:

- *Distributed social practices and digital uses of social networks:* Teachers have created networks by school subjects, professional interests, in primary and secondary education.
- *A strategy for change:* In a context of school restructuring and education reforms and of evolution of curricula and the teaching profession, there is need for a supportive environment and a new sense of professionalism. The RESPIRE national network has been designed to support the fluidity of professional relationships. It belongs within the national strategy of innovation by contributing the knowledge bank of innovations (*Expérithèque* – more than 2 500 innovations already compiled and updated http://eduscol.education.fr/experitheque). It is supported by a national network of school development partners who are sustaining the initiatives, supporting teaching teams, and implementing a national programme of professional development based on self-evaluation.
- Creating *"communities of practice"*: RESPIRE facilitates the development of communities of practice and professional learning communities through the provision of a new social mediation of knowledge between practitioners. By this means, knowledge and experiences, experiments and initiatives, projects and best practices are shared and disseminated.

RESPIRE embodies four principles embedded in the interface, exchanges and contributions involving approximately 5 000 interconnected persons:

- *Informality:* The expression is free and explicit, without any level of validation required; different supports such as forums and blogs allow people to interact quickly and effectively, with sustainable and relevant content.
- *Personalisation:* Each contributor is identified and navigates according to his/her own interests and questions. Interactions are focused and shared at the same time.
- *Open source:* Knowledge is easily shared, or delimited according to the desired level of publicity.
- *Co-operation:* Each group can share questions and answers, resources and documents; the rationale is transversal and collaborative and not top-down.

The RESPIRE network is inspired by several types of networks and cannot be reduced to one. It serves as a social network in education with strong institutional support. RESPIRE is "a network for professional exchanges in innovation, research, and experiment"(http://respire-education.fr) and it helps make accessible an emergent national and professional learning community and knowledge about the main challenges of the French education system.

Source: France Notes, http://www.oecd.org/edu/ceri/implementationandchange.htm.

Platforms are prominent among the strategies submitted to the OECD/ILE project. The French innovation platform *Respire* (Box 3.4) organised by the National Ministry of Education, has gathered more than 2 500 innovations and the platform hosts communities of practice. It is organised around four guiding principles: informality, personalisation, open source and co-operation. It thus facilitates factors that already have an existence – the digital use of social networks, a strategy for change, and a community of practice – and breathes life into them. The "Mother Tongue Theme Site" has been running since 2001, co-ordinated and managed by the Swedish National Agency for Education. In 2003, it won the award for the Best Global Website for "the most innovative multilingual and multicultural site in Europe". One hundred teachers and school leaders contribute to the site with unique content in 45 different languages, and the website has three parts: general information, online resources and language rooms. It is actively linked to professional development activities – conferences, seminars and training courses.

The Finnish National Board of Education launched a new portal as an open service at the end of 2012 to facilitate the spread of innovation and good practices; learning environments is one of the themes included in the portal. The *Enlaces* programme organised by the Chilean Ministry of Education has developed online resources on quality and innovative pedagogical practices, and provides syntheses and associated teacher resources. Technology is a key part of the KwaZulu-Natal initiative in South Africa – ICT in Education using child-centred teaching and learning. The British Columbia Networks for Inquiry and Innovation use blogs, wikis and the web as their lifeblood. In South Australia, one of three main DECD strategies is about transforming schools to make the best use of emerging technology, and with an innovations website as a core resource.

UNETE is a business association in Mexico aimed at introducing technology into teaching and learning in schools. UNETE partners with some 7 500 schools altogether. As well as offering technological support, it has created an educational portal *ComunidadUNETE*, designed to address teachers' needs and concerns. It gathers international and national educational content that teachers can use, grade, discuss, share and recommend to other colleagues and students. *ComunidadUNETE* also promotes information and content exchange through the Teacher Network within the portal, with forums and virtual communities for collaboration, meetings and discussion of different topics. There is a year-long intensive personal mentorship programme, with remote mentorship for up to three years, supplemented by capacity building and professional development. With approximately 29 000 different users *ComunidadUNETE* is one of the most used channels means of communication among principals and teachers in Mexico.

The NMS development in Austria is supported by an online platform, comprising some 200 eduMoodle courses, which is operated by the National Centre for Virtual Teacher Education (Onlinecampus VPH) in co-operation with the Centre for Learning Schools (CLS) and the NMS eLearning strategic unit. In addition, the NMS Online Library serves as a portal for NMS-related resources, including dissemination of the newest resources for curriculum and instruction developed by CLS, a biweekly newsletter for school principals and a series of online events and publications called "NMS Insights". There is also the "Meta-Course", the virtual networking and learning space for all *Lerndesigners*. This is closed to visitors so that it can be a safe place to exchange ideas and developments. It has become Austria's most active educational platform.

Online materials and exchanges may be used to enhance autonomy and flexibility or they may be used to standardise. The Teacher Resource Centre (TRC) in the Innova Schools network in Peru is the online home for a wide set of quality lessons, authored by the network, and aligned to the grade standards and termly learning outcomes, for each subject across every grade. Their aggregation as one central resource is viewed as a way to distribute quality teaching resources throughout the network, to simplify lesson planning, and to create standard-based lessons across the Innova Schools network. It is also hoped thereby to create a community of practice where teachers can build on the initial materials and upload and share new resources.

Box 3.5. **Peru: Innova Schools – Sustainable change, lessons from the private sector**

Innova Schools, a network of private schools in Peru, has developed a viable model to offer high quality and affordable education to middle class learners. It started as a full-fledged company in 2010 with the plan to build a nationwide network of 70 schools that should serve over 70 000 students by 2020. Today, the network is operating 22 schools, 18 in the peripheral areas of the capital city of Lima, and 4 in the provinces. Partnerships at the national and international levels with the private sector (Intercorp, IDEO), universities (PUCP and Cayetano Herrera universities) and educational organisations (such as the Ontario Principals' Council) are key for the sustainable growth of this network. Innova is also developing strong relationships with the Peruvian Ministry of Education.

The network's pedagogical model aims to: prepare learners to become actors of change in Peru by developing their leadership, 21st century skills and ethical and human values; meet international standards of quality; and promote lifelong learning.

The content in these learning environments goes beyond the Peruvian mandated curriculum and includes standards based on educational models in Australia, Canada, Chile and Colombia. Since 2014, the Understanding by Design (UbD) framework has inspired a process of curriculum innovation.

There is a mix of two learning methods being used: "Group Learning" (frontal teaching in the classroom with socio-constructivist approach) and "Solo Learning" (virtual, autonomous, self-paced learning in the technology rooms). In addition, cross-subject and cross-grade inquiry projects called "Innovation Programs" take place on a yearly basis. In 2014, a new pedagogical approach "Flipped Learning" was piloted in two schools. Students prepare in advance by doing research at home on a topic to be covered at school. The teacher then guides a discussion and learners do guided "homework" in the classroom.

Innova is not only a network of schools, but has a system-like functioning model with different departments ensuring quality and sustainability in: teacher training and monitoring (young teachers engaged and trained by Innova and its partner universities, and monitored through their practice); evaluation and accountability (of learning outcomes, teacher performance, parents satisfaction and system functioning); scalability (future projection, architecture, resources);and innovation and pedagogy (constant revision of the pedagogical model and innovation opportunities system-wide).

Source: Innova Schools (Peru) Notes, http://www.oecd.org/edu/ceri/implementationandchange.htm.

In short, platforms and digital communications have become a prominent part of strategies to grow and sustain innovative learning environments, albeit that this can take many different forms.

Change agents

A number of the strategies involve the creation through policy initiatives of specific change agents, who are able to exercise influence at the local level and help to sustain the drive to innovation. Austria's *Lerndesigners* in the NMS reform is a new teacher leadership role, seen as complementary to the leadership of principals and senior managers while not replacing it. This is not only an individual role: networking and learning are made possible through their periodic *lernateliers* and the *Lerndesigners* have established a nationwide community of practice to ensure that they can act as effective change agents. The Itinerant Pedagogical Advisors (*Conafe*, Mexico) have been created specifically as advisors to contribute to the improvement of learning in schools working with *Conafe* in communities where existing educational resources are weak. School co-ordinators in the Curricular Integration of Key Competences project in Spain became the leaders of this strategy in each school as did the leaders in Slovenia's "Renovation through School Development Teams". Norway created a cadre of "Advisory Teams" aimed at supporting those running schools in problematic areas of achievement and quality. The Thuringian innovation has also relied on a set of school-based innovation leaders – the counsellors for school development.

Box 3.6. **Austria: School reform through change agents**

The Austrian school reform initiative "New Secondary School" (NMS) began in 2008 in 67 pilot schools and has since led to a mandated school reform for the whole sector to be completed in phases by 2018. By the 2013/14 school year, the 6th generation of participating schools started in 254 school sites. The goal of NMS is to foster innovative learning environments and equity in the lower secondary sector. The pilot phase initiated and implemented networks and communities of practice at all system levels. The focus is on school principals and *Lerndesigners* – a teacher leadership role, new for Austria, to act as change agents and provide leverage for school reform. The rationale is clear: school reform must happen at the school level and change agents require networking and communities of practice.

Each NMS school designates a member of the teaching staff to be the *Lerndesigner*, who attends national and regional network meetings. To strengthen the role and foster innovation, school principals were also invited to a national network meeting each semester to address their own leadership and develop shared approaches with the *Lerndesigners* as part of the change strategy.

A two-year qualification programme (*lernateliers*) is provided by the University Colleges of Teacher Education in co-operation with the newly-established National Centre for Learning Schools (CLS) and focuses on teacher leadership and professional learning in six areas (the "NMS-House": mindfulness of learning, difference and diversity, competence orientation, "backwards design" curriculum development, differentiated instruction, and assessment). To sustain positive change and foster learning environments which are equitable and challenging for all NMS lower secondary pupils, the CLS has the following primary objectives:

- sustain and foster school networks and communities of practice
- develop change agents through qualification programmes, symposia and networking
- integrate findings from current learning research into the NMS environment and development strategies
- disseminate next practice insights and examples online and in print
- support change processes in teacher education to meet the goals of the NM
- exploit system-wide synergy potentials
- provide support for policy and program development.

Responding to the need to connect *Lerndesigners*, virtual Professional Learning Communities (PLCs) have been in a prototyping phase since the school year 2013/14 and are now being implemented as common practice. With the aim of exploring the impact of *Lerndesigners'* digital networking, virtual PLC sessions are captured in "vignettes", short (10-20 lines) descriptions of key experiences. Rather than summarising content, vignettes focus on recreating participants' experiences by capturing the emotions and events emerging during the session. Deep understanding of their practice and new ways of thinking appear frequently in the vignettes alongside with problems like coping with technology or making the time to attend the sessions. These vignettes are used as evidence to inform the CLS on the learning impact and needed improvements of the PLC sessions.

Source: Austria Notes, http://www.oecd.org/edu/ceri/implementationandchange.htm.

The examples are by no means identical – some are about advisors to principals, others are teacher leaders, others are specific learning coaches and consultants – while sharing the feature of being newly-created roles to meet needs that call for specialist knowledge and functioning. There may be tensions and trade-offs in the degree of formalisation of such roles: the greater the formalisation the greater their recognition and the tighter the processes yet at the risk of reducing local flexibility and of increasing resistance. It may be that roles need time to be formalised and embedded rather than introduced wholesale from the beginning.

Main summary highlights

This chapter provides an overview of the strategies and initiatives that were contributed to the "implementation and change" strand of the ILE study. Altogether, 26 countries, provincial states and foundation networks submitted examples of promising change strategies. Several of these have been directly led and organised by the national ministry of education but in others it has had a support role or else the initiative is not a national one or it is being led from elsewhere altogether. Some only cover a relatively small network while others are going system-wide, with most in-between.

They provide a rich set of cases from which to gain insights into the range of approaches being taken to spread and sustain innovative learning in different systems around the world but they represent only a tiny number of the possible initiatives and strategies that might have been considered. They can thus make no claim to be "best practice" and indeed it is doubtful that any strategy deserves to be identified as "global best practice".

The chapter identifies a set of underlying threads that run through the diverse strategies and initiatives, which are summarised as a series of **C's**:

- *Culture change:* Several of the strategies emphasise the importance of creating culture change in schools as more important than surface change but also much more difficult to realise.

- *Clarifying focus:* Many of the innovation strategies reported to OECD/ILE are aimed right at such mainstream goals as addressing low educational achievement and enhancing quality. Innovation is necessary because repeating variants of conventional approaches has failed to dent the problems.

  Clear focus is the opposite of "letting 1000 flowers bloom" and trying to cover everything all at once risks disjointed diffusion of effort and missing all targets in the process. Choices often need to be made while avoiding the narrow goal-setting that blinkers wider innovation.

- *Capacity creation – knowledge, professional learning:* A common cornerstone is the need to generate knowledge about the student learning that is taking place, and for that knowledge to be acted upon. Professional learning and thereby capacity creation go hand-in-hand with knowledge in strategies to spread innovative learning environments.

  A research component is often needed to understand how a strategy might be optimised and to create the materials to do so through such means as teacher education and leadership. The creation of expert knowledge and converting that into accessible forms and formats may call for specialist institutes for this purpose.

- *Collaboration and cooperation:* Collaborative professionalism is assumed in many of the strategies for growing and sustaining innovative learning as are networks and professional learning communities based on collaboration and co-operation.

  Networks are based on voluntary and motivated engagement rather than obligation and may thus seem ephemeral compared with well-defined educational structures. In fact, networking is becoming the natural form of collective action in contemporary learning systems. There is a clear policy role in helping to establish the climate and means for effective networking.

- *Communication technologies and platforms:* Platforms and digital communications have become a prominent part of strategies to grow and sustain innovative learning environments, albeit that this can take many different forms. The platform may be the main strategy or more a means to facilitate communication.

- *Change agents:* A number of the strategies involve the creation through policy initiatives of specific change agents, who are able to exercise influence on the ground and provide the expertise and drive to sustain the innovation. There may be tensions and trade-offs in the optimal degree of formalisation of such roles.

References

Bentley, T. and S. Gillinson (2007), *A D&R System for Education*, Innovation Unit, London.

Cheng, E.C.K and M.L. Mo (2013), "The approach of Learning Study: Its origin and implications", *OECD Education Working Papers*, No. 94, OECD Publishing, Paris, http://dx.doi.org/10.1787/5k3wjp0s959p-en.

Dumont, H., D. Istance, and F. Benavides (2010), *The Nature of Learning: Using Research to Inspire Practice*, Educational Research and Innovation, OECD Publishing, Paris, http://dx.doi.org/10.1787/9789264086487-en.

Istance, D. and M. Kools (2013), "OECD work on technology and education: Innovative learning environments as an integrating framework", *European Journal of Education*, Vol. 48, No.1, March, pp. 43-57.

Jolonch, A., M. Martinez and J. Badia (2013), "Promoting learning leadership in Catalonia and beyond", in *Leadership for 21st Century Learning*, OECD Publishing, Paris, http://dx.doi.org/10.1787/9789264205406-8-en.

OECD (2015), "Growing and sustaining innovative learning environments", in *Education Policy Outlook 2015: Making Reforms Happen*, OECD Publishing, Paris, Chapter 8, http://dx.doi.org/10.1787/9789264225442-12-en.

OECD (2013a), *Innovative Learning Environments*, Educational Research and Innovation, OECD Publishing, Paris, http://dx.doi.org/10.1787/9789264203488-en.

OECD (2013b), *Leadership for 21st Century Learning*, Educational Research and Innovation, OECD Publishing, Paris, http://dx.doi.org/10.1787/9789264205406-en.

OECD (2009), *Working Out Change: Systemic Innovation in Vocational Education and Training*, Educational Research and Innovation, OECD Publishing, Paris, http://dx.doi.org/10.1787/9789264075924-en.

OECD, (2004), *Innovation in the Knowledge Economy: Implications for Education and Learning*, Educational Research and Innovation, OECD Publishing, Paris, http://dx.doi.org/10.1787/9789264105621-en.

Resnick, L. B., P. J. Spillane, P. Goldman and E. S. Rangel (2010), "Implementing innovation: From visionary models to everyday practice", in *The Nature of Learning: Using Research to Inspire Practice*, OECD Publishing, Paris, pp. 285-315, http://dx.doi.org/10.1787/9789264086487-14-en.

Chapter 4

Growing innovative learning through meso-level networking

The strategies and initiatives featured in the ILE study are operating at the "meso" level, and their differing scale is described in this chapter. While networks and initiatives are constantly emerging and evolving, they often disappear as well. Growth depends on the emergence of healthy new learning-focused networks outstripping the inevitable decline or disappearance of others. The chapter extends the ILE framework architecture to accommodate the meso level and uses this to present the submitted strategies and initiatives: the degree to which they are learning-focused; their balance of the formal and non-formal; and the means of diffusion and innovation "contagion". As well as extending the ILE framework, the chapter also uses the framework to ask how well the initiatives are applying it to themselves: how are these strategies applying the lessons of learning principles, designing and redesigning on the basis of learning evidence, and bringing in different partners in their operationalisation?

This chapter looks in more detail at the way the initiatives and strategies submitted to the ILE project contribute to broader innovative eco-systems of learning. They do this directly and indirectly. Directly, such initiatives populate systems with new forms of collective innovation primarily through creating different networks, chains and communities, formal and non-formal. Hence, the submitted strategies and initiatives are operating at the meso level. Indirectly, they are offering inspiring examples for shifting cultures and dominant policy assumptions and so are about changing climates. They are contributing to what some see as the "innovation epidemic" (Hargreaves 2003), shifting dominant values and practices through the contagion of ideas and innovations.

The different strategies and initiatives submitted to the ILE project are far from exhaustive of the range of different networks and approaches but they illustrate dimensions that help to capture the meso level:

- How *learning focused?* (The extent to which learning is front and centre of the network or community of practice – why and what?)
- How *horizontally spread to include the non-formal?* (The extent of involvement of non-formal relationships and players – who?)
- How *do they connect and diffuse?* (The methods used to spread innovative ideas and practices and how effective these methods are – how? how well?)

These dimensions structure this chapter, richly illustrated by the submitted strategies and initiatives. We conclude the chapter by exploring how some work in ways that are consistent with the 7+3 framework itself.

As networks, communities of practice and strategies are constantly emerging and evolving, inevitably they often disappear as well – naturally in organic eco-systems as opposed to permanent structures. Therefore, growth depends on the emergence of healthy new learning-focused networks being sustained and outstripping the inevitable decline or disappearance of others. This system characteristic of the dynamic balance of growth and decline comes into sharper relief once the focus shifts from the single learning environment to wider systems and once the trajectories of initiatives are examined instead of seeing policies through snapshots. These perspectives have been integral to the final phase of the ILE project including the ambition to follow certain initiatives over time. By the end of the international study, a number of those submitted had been absorbed into others or had disappeared altogether.

The strategies and initiatives as meso-level innovation

The different strategies are primarily meso-level initiatives even when they have ambitions to influence or arrive at whole system change (the figures reported in this section refer to scale at the time the country reports were drafted which, of course, may have altered since then). This feature of the strategies and initiatives submitted to the OECD/ILE project is not immediately obvious, but it is fundamental to the nature of change in larger eco-systems of learning. And if there are system-wide ambitions for the initiative to lead wider transformation, there is the question to consider of how this is expected to take place (taken up in Chapter 5).

In British Columbia (Canada), 156 individual schools in 44 districts are active members of *Networks of Inquiry and Innovation* (NOII) and the *Aboriginal Enhancement Schools Network* (AESN). The *Whole Education Network* in England (United Kingdom) is a growing membership network currently of some 150 schools with partners who share its values drawn from both third sector and other organisations. In Israel, each year 15 new experimental schools join the Education Ministry's Experiments and Entrepreneurship Division innovation programme, while 15 others complete their five-year experimental period and function independently again. In any given year, 80 experimental schools are operating simultaneously under the aegis of this innovation strategy. Since 1996 it has nurtured over 300 experimental schools, and today supports 37 diffusion centres. The ILE project in KwaZulu-Natal (South Africa) encompasses 196 schools spread across three districts.

Larger scale may be achieved – approximately twice as many sites in the following examples. The French Belgian initiative "*Décolâge!*" had by April 2014 grown to include 300 schools (1 in 6 of that system's schools) and 75 social centres (1 in 2), with over 800 teachers having taken the associated training. The New Zealand *Learning and Change Network Strategy* has led to the creation of nearly 60 separate Learning and Change Network (LCN) networks (57), involving approximately 15% of the country's schools/kura. In some initiatives, relative numbers are larger still, such as Finland's On the Move! – at the time of writing, the number of schools participating in the programme was 500, and the aim is to expand it further to cover all Finnish schools.

Box 4.1. **British Columbia (Canada): Meso-level strategies combine**

1) Spirals of Inquiry: The disciplined approach to inquiry is informing and shaping the transformative work in schools and districts across the province. Participating schools engage in a year-long period to focus on inquiry learning using the Spiral of Inquiry as the framework with six key stages: scanning, focusing, developing a hunch, new professional learning, taking action and checking that a big enough difference has been made. At each stage, three key questions are asked: What is going on for our learners? How do we know this? How does this matter? Thirty-six school districts (60% of the total) are involved directly in specific leadership development based on the Spiral of Inquiry.

2) Certificate in Innovative Educational Leadership (CIEL): The leadership programme at Vancouver Island University brings together educational leaders in formal and non-formal positions. The programme has an emphasis on: i) understanding and applying the Spiral of Inquiry; ii) exploring, analysing and applying ideas from innovative cases gathered by the OECD/ILE project; and iii) becoming knowledgeable about the seven OECD/ILE Learning Principles. To date, three cohorts with a total of over 100 have graduated, with 30 more enrolled in 2014-2015. CIEL graduates are working as formal or informal leaders in 26 school districts.

3) Networks of Inquiry and Innovation (NOII) and the Aboriginal Enhancement Schools Network (AESN): These networks connect professional learning through principals, teachers and support staff and accelerate the transformative work across the province. To date, 156 individual schools in 44 districts in BC are active members of NOII and AESN. A grant from the Federal Government funded a research study on the impact of teacher involvement in AES and examined more than 50 inquiry projects around the province. The focus on inquiry learning has proved to be beneficial to the Aboriginal and non-Aboriginal students and teachers, as the model starts by analysing the interests and needs of the last. The AESN is considered to be an effective mechanism for sustainable teaching and learning change.

BC is in the midst of redesigning the curriculum and assessment framework, in which several graduates from the CIEL leadership programme are involved. These three strategies create a "third space" that is not dominated by provincial or local politics, even if financial support from the government is involved. It is a grass-roots professional initiative, regulated by meso-level leadership and looking to bring in sustainable change for the entire province.

Source: British Columbia (Canada) Notes, http://www.oecd.org/edu/ceri/implementationandchange.htm.

Not all enjoy such a wide take-up. In the Thuringian *ILE start-up project* (Germany), the learning environments of 33 Thuringian schools from across the state are being systematically enhanced over an initial period of 3 years. *Innova Schools* in Peru is working towards creating a nationwide network of 70 schools that are intended to serve over 70 000 students by 2020, of which 22 were in operation in 2014. Fifteen South Australian Department for Education and Child Development (DECD) schools, preschools and an early childhood programme constituted the state-wide *Innovation Community of Practice* even if, as we see in Chapter 5, the aim was to influence wider change.

We have compared scale here to illustrate how such initiatives are populating the meso level of the larger learning system. But they are, of course, very different, and this chapter elaborates how they vary around key dimensions.

Extending the learning system architecture

This section presents an extended ILE architecture for understanding learning systems when the focus is beyond the single environment. When the focus so widens, it is necessary to include the institutional components and infrastructure, the verticality of formal governance and the horizontality of the voluntary and non-formal, and the connections of knowledge and collaboration that bind the learning system elements together. So far we have made the ILE framework "institution-neutral" as the learning environment as we have defined it may be found in a wide variety of different institutional forms. But in describing the architecture of learning eco-systems, we need to be able to distinguish different organisational forms and identify descriptive features which characterise the kind of learning system it is.

A variety of elements could be identified to describe a meso-level eco-learning system such as size, degree of regulation, institutional/organisational membership, resourcing, and technology infrastructure. There is then the nature of the connections linking these different elements and purposes. In this chapter, we condense these down to a small number of dimensions to capture the nature of particular networks and meso-level strategies. These dimensions can also open up the question of the effectiveness of different arrangements:

- *Learning focused:* How learning focused is the network, and how far focused on innovative learning as defined in ILE work through the seven principles?
- *Balance of formal and non-formal:* How networked are formal learning environments in non-formal ways? How active and visible are non-formal learning environments? How far are there mixed ("hybrid") formal and non-formal arrangements? This is also to address the extent of horizontality of learning systems around the vertical governance structures of formal school systems.
- *The means of innovation "contagion":* The meso-level grouping serves as the vehicle for spreading learning innovation, drawing on the examples, support and co-operation of others undertaking similar learning journeys within the network. The nature of the diffusion within networks is thus critical.

A networked initiative or chain may itself be innovating its understanding of pedagogical relationships, content and resources, have an active design leadership using learning evidence, and be reaching out to other bodies or networks. That is, it may as a whole be applying the ILE framework in its operation and we look at this to conclude the chapter.

Strengthening the focus on 21st century learning

The initiatives and strategies discussed in this report are already particular in being skewed towards 21st century learning (otherwise they would not have engaged with the OECD/ILE study). From that broad common starting point, however, they differ in the extent to which they are explicitly learning focused, the particular learning aims they are seeking to achieve, and how they are working in practice to put learning at the centre. Sometimes indeed the focus on learning has strengthened as the strategy has been implemented. On the Move! in Finland, for instance, is a programme that has put learning increasingly at the heart of its rationale. When it began, the main focus was on the relationship between physical activity among young people and health. As it has evolved the focus has increasingly embraced the positive effects of a physically active culture on the learning environment.

Assessing the learning challenge

The New Zealand Learning and Change Networks (LCN) have developed a set of tools to reinforce network activity around a close understanding of achievement challenges with the prominent engagement of young people and their families/whānau and communities, and not just the professionals. Leaders articulate hunches about priority achievement challenges and then check the views of students, teachers and families/whānau; students map their current learning environments; and students, teachers, families/whānau and leaders analyse the strengths, supports and achievement challenges. Out of these come change priorities at both school and network levels. Two types of evaluation have taken place: evaluative probes and specific evaluation of academic outcomes and practice changes within networks. The evaluative probes have been to: i) support leadership decisions about focus, ii) check how far the network's preferred change priorities match the strategy intent; and iii) assess breadth of understanding and coherence of thinking in making the changes. The Ministry of Education's Network Capability Tools have been created to support network leadership groups to monitor and measure their network leadership capability so as to empower them to check on coherence between network and school change actions, and the impact of change actions on student achievement. In other words, the LCN strategy has been very strongly focused on learning itself, engaging all members of each learning community and the community created by the network, with explicit and formalised tools to underpin this strong learning focus.

The "Spirals of Enquiry" applied in the British Columbia Networks start similarly with scanning student learning to give the launch pad for activity and collaboration. The result is widespread change in student learning, among both Aboriginal and non-Aboriginal learners. One research study examined more than 50 inquiry projects around the province in how they traced and assessed the impacts of their inquiries on student learning. The network provides a structure and a process for systematically collecting written summaries of this work into the case study format promoted by the network leaders in each district. The cases illustrate in concrete form how teachers went about improving their practice and investigating ways in which learning might be better realised: "As such, the cases provide a remarkable record of and a database for documenting and building on initial investigations." (McGregor, 2013: 122)

In the French Community of Belgium, there has long been the creation of pedagogical tools, distributed to schools through booklets sent to schools, and through pedagogical resources available on the ministry website. But now *Décolâge!* has created "a complete and coherent pedagogical kit" to underscore how much learning and appropriate pedagogy are at the core. The ILE "Practitioner Guide" booklet, based on the 2010 publication *The Nature of Learning*, has also been translated into French by *Décolâge!* and made available to participants.

Interpreting 21st century learning

The aims of the British Columbia (BC) strategy can be summarised around three defining goals that have emerged over the past decade of work with networks of schools. First, there is the aim to change the learning environment for *every* young person in BC through more intellectually engaging, flexible, responsive and informed learning and teaching. Second, there needs to be a priority focus specifically on the outcomes for Aboriginal learners and on engaging with Aboriginal history, knowledge and culture by everyone connected with the education system. Third, networked educators want to ensure that learning environments will lead to sustained curiosity, inquiry-mindedness and an interest in learning for a lifetime. Hence, as well as a generalised focus on learning, this is interpreted in specific ways around engagement, equity and laying foundations for lifelong learning.

In line with developing key competences for lifelong learning, *Innova Schools* in Peru has developed a student learning profile that signals the competences that students are expected to have at the end of their school life, based on a defined set of core competences with associated means of acquiring those competences (effective communication; effective communication in English; mathematical competence; scientific thought; able use of technology; leadership, entrepreneurship and initiatives; autonomy; collaboration; creative expression; and social and civic awareness).

The Slovenian initiative on Renovating Schooling through School Development Teams has specified what is needed to put learning at the centre, with an agenda that closely matches many definitions of 21st century learning and competence:

- to encourage the use of process and problem-solving approaches to learning
- to foster higher-order thinking and competency development
- to encourage a wider repertoire of teaching and assessment methods and strategies
- to establish interdisciplinary and cross-disciplinary connections and promote elements of an integrated curriculum
- to enhance the authenticity of learning situations
- to identify solutions to organisational issues that will support renewed forms of teaching and learning.

"The Framework for External Evaluation in Baden-Württemberg" (Germany) in essence offers the criteria that define the learning to be promoted. In the latest version of the "Framework", personalised learning has been added as a new criterion. The question of appropriate and new metrics is thus tackled, and how a school succeeds at providing both group-specific and personalised learning opportunities is now taken as an important reflection of the quality of its teaching.

The Experimental Schools in Israel are expected to provide students with learning environments that support and develop academic achievements as well as social values within a pedagogically innovative and nurturing school culture; all this while responding to the widespread Israeli perception of what is a successful school: high achievements, a positive school environment and a good reputation. Hence, innovation is encouraged but within the broad parameters of what is understood to constitute good schooling.

Three 21st century learning models and designs

UNETE (Mexico) created a new network for teachers, principals, and students aimed at *innovating pedagogical cores*. Before, many teachers did not have a support system beyond their own community. UNETE connects teachers with other teachers throughout the country; it creates in-classroom partnerships between students where learning was once an individual undertaking. This also helps students, teachers and parents understand the relevance of curriculum outside of the classroom. In line with the ILE framework, UNETE helps teachers learn to embrace challenge and alternative ways of teaching by supporting them, and giving them access to new content and information. Through building trust with teachers, UNETE can evaluate the effectiveness of its programmes, and teachers can see that evaluation is a step to better teaching and learning, as opposed to an action leading to reprimand. Additionally, UNETE works closely with principals and community leaders to develop champions of new ways of learning and improved education. UNETE facilitates intensive partnerships among teachers, their principals, and communities, and works with federal, state and municipal governments to implement the programmes and foster sustainability. Students partner more with their classmates and with their families by bringing home knowledge relevant to the lives of those in their households.

Innova Schools (Peru) is seeking to shift from teacher-centred schools, in which teachers' knowledge is basically transmitted to students, to schools that are learner-centred. Students actively engage and interact with different sources of learning – e-books, internet, the teacher, other classmates, with guidelines provided by their teachers – with technology regarded as an important tool facilitated by teachers. A social constructivist learning model allows students to seek knowledge and construct their own understanding. It is costly to achieve, however, and is demanding on teachers, and both are barriers to scale. Teachers need robust pedagogy and to be confident in the discipline. They need self-confidence to elaborate on student questions and engage in discussion, and to be open to different ways of student reasoning. It needs strong teacher training, teacher mentoring and not very large groups or classes. Innova Schools uses guiding principles summarising shared understandings of both the nature of learning and the nature of teaching. Technology is not only a tool, but is seen as the most important vehicle for learning and teaching, giving students the opportunities to achieve to a high level. Figure 4.1 shows how the relationships are viewed between the learner, the pedagogical core guiding principles and the role of technology.

Figure 4.1. **The Innova Schools (Peru) model**

The IS learner	Guiding principles	Role of technology
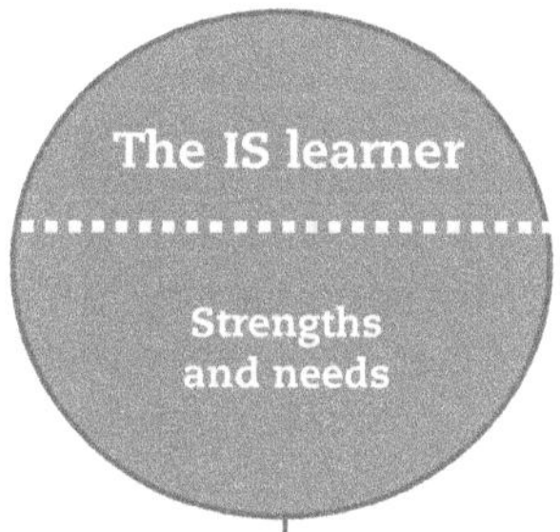 The IS learner Strengths and needs	• Students are able to build their own learning • Learning is a social construction • Learning starts with demands that come from students´ real context • Learning should be meaningful • Students should be highly engaged in learning tasks • Learning involves both the intellectual and ethical dimensions of students • Learning through discovery	• Technology changes the process of learning • Students will lead a deep change in the way knowledge is addressed in schools • Technology can give us more information about student achievement • Technology provides us strong simulations about real life phenomena • Technology allow us to meet the specific needs of each student

Technology changes and enhances learning – teaching processes

Source: Innova Schools (Peru) Notes, http://www.oecd.org/edu/ceri/implementationandchange.htm.

Different models embed technology in the learning process, especially blended learning and flipped instruction. Blended learning combines direct hands-on experiences in the classroom with digital learning in which students use computer-based tools to discover and work through core academic concepts. It combines face-to-face interaction in learning spaces with technology where students are working one to one with an electronic device. This takes two forms at Innova Schools: group learning and solo learning.

- In *group learning* students collaborate with each other, often in small groups that are led by a teacher to discover new concepts and develop higher-order understanding through projects and exercises. While group learning is key to helping students develop academic knowledge, it also supports the development of competences such as collaboration, teamwork and leadership. This usually happens in classes of around 30 students.

- *Solo learning* is independent, student-led and self-paced learning often enabled by technology. Students construct their own goals, paths and work flows, with teachers providing targeted support as needed; they learn to develop autonomy, focus and responsibility for their own learning. Solo learning usually happens in groups of around 60 students.

The flipped instruction model is a form of blended learning in which students learn new content on line, watching videos or interacting with digital resources, usually at home. What used to be the assigned problems of homework are then done in class with teachers offering more personalised guidance, scaffolding and interaction with students. At home, the students explore content that turns into prior knowledge that they will later use in the classroom. It allows students to address higher-order thinking tasks in the classroom. The more robust is the prior knowledge the greater the possibilities to transfer and apply it to new and different situations. This is still in its early stages of implementation.

Similarly, the learning arrangements in the innovative schools in the South Australian network are consistent with the ILE framework in relation to "learners", "educators", "content", "resources", and "organisation and pedagogy". The South Australian sites are innovating with their learners – for example, by operating with multi-age groupings such as reception to year 7 "Magpie" groupings and year 10-12 tutor groups – and innovating content, with big picture and "fertile questions" being used to stimulate interdisciplinary and deep learning experiences. Regarding organisation and pedagogy, individual student learning plans feature prominently in the innovation sites as do restructured timetables and targeted student groups. Innovation in resources is found in newly-built, purpose-built facilities or when traditional physical spaces have been renovated, with transformed areas being "campfires" for targeted master classes and specialist skill-building, or "cave spaces" for quiet reflection. Regarding educators as activators, facilitators, coaches and mentors, they meet regularly and then typically engage in co-planning, co-teaching and co-assessing, while also considering data and other evidence about individual student progress (Owen, 2012).

The question of how "learning focused" is the strategy or initiative and what this means in detail thus goes deeply into the philosophies and dynamics of the different strategies and systems and their chosen modes of innovation. What stands out among several of the networked initiatives in the ILE study is the importance given to identifying the learning challenge at the outset, rather than this being taken as known, and the role played by learners and their families in this process. Variants around 21st century competence define the learning aims of those initiatives, but also respect and knowledge of cultural values – a further reminder that innovation does not always mean to introduce something new but may be needed to come back to traditional knowledge and values. The networked strategies may then have more or less elaborated designs that incorporate pedagogies and different approaches to teaching, learning and assessment in holistic models. Hence, to describe a networked strategy as "learning focused" in fact covers a wide range of different approaches and choices in combination, including how explicit and shared are the designs that underpin them across the different sites that come together at the meso level.

Horizontality through different combinations of the formal and non-formal

Most of the initiatives submitted to the ILE project are school-based. They are thus clustered towards the formal end of the spectrum and this is partly due to the nature of participation in this international study which facilitated engagement by education authorities. Yet more generally, different mixes of formal and non-formal may be involved in initiatives to grow and sustain innovative learning. Being able to specify the mix of formal and non-formal in meso networks and grouping permits clarification of the relationship to the established educational authorities and resources and, when the different meso networks are aggregated, help to ascertain the composition of the meta learning system.

We might distinguish four forms of networking and clustering that vary regarding the mix of formal and non-formal:

i) There may be formal initiatives that bring schools into clusters and networks, thereby developing the meso level through combining schools in a particular jurisdiction that otherwise would be working in isolation.

ii) There may be networks of schools and school-based communities of practice that develop through initiatives that are voluntary, and so not relying on the requirements of their education authorities to form clusters.

iii) There may be initiatives for formal schools to work increasingly with different community bodies and non-formal sources of teaching and learning, not only in the partnerships developed by individual learning environments but by groups of such schools creating more systemic partnership arrangements.

iv) There may be purely non-formal initiatives that come into the learning space which rely neither on schools within the official school system, and may not operate through recognisably school institutions at all.

The ILE cases tend to be oriented towards the formal end of the spectrum, covering i), ii) and iii). For example, the Whole Education Network in England (WEN) is a growing membership network currently of some 150 schools and thus may be seen to belong to ii), but also it works with partners who share its values drawn from both third sector and other organisations – i.e. iii) – including the RSA (Royal Society for the Encouragement of Arts, Manufactures and Commerce). Whole Education is a not-for-profit organisation based in London that grew out of an RSA charter. Its primary aims are to develop a network to enable schools to provide a high quality, whole education and to argue the need for and impact of a whole education.

The French Belgian initiative *Décolage!* had 300 schools engaged in April 2014 but, with its focus on early childhood, it also had involved about half (75) of the psycho-medico-social centres in this educational community as well. In Finland's "On the Move" initiative to improve the health and well-being of Finnish young people, the municipalities and schools build their own local networks and these extend well beyond schools. These usually include municipal bodies (e.g. youth, health, sports, leisure sectors) and various associations and organisations (e.g. sports associations) representing the tertiary sector and also parents and their associations. At the national level, important partners have been the Young Finland Association (*Nuori Suomi*) which was a national association to promote well-being and quality of life of children and young people through physical activity and sports (activities now transferred to Valo).

Box 4.2. **Innolukio ("innovative general upper secondary school"), Finland**

This grew from a small local initiative to a nationwide venture in which the main focus was on entrepreneurship.

"Innolukio learning environment encourages upper secondary school students towards creative thinking and provides them with the knowledge and skills that are required in future work tasks. The essential goal of the project is to create a connection between upper secondary school students, businesses and universities, while utilising the creativity of the students as a national resource. The Innolukio concept encompasses, for example, inspirational videos, weekly exercises, the Innolukio competition and other learning materials that support creativity. The learning environment is free-of-charge to upper secondary schools and their students. Students are primarily intended to engage in the activities during their free-time, but teachers can freely use the materials for teaching purposes."

The initiative started in a single school in a small town in the Northern Finland (Ylievieska). Several years later, at the beginning of the 2012/13 school year, the network included 320 upper secondary schools and 110 000 students. As it has transformed since, it has been spreading to vocational upper secondary schools and polytechnics and now comprehensive schools as well.

The partners for "Innolukio" included the Finnish National Board of Education, the Ministry of Employment and Economy, the Trade Union of Education in Finland, the Association of Finnish Local and Regional Authorities, Aalto University, University of Oulu, the Federation of Finnish Technology Industries, the Economic Information Office, Nokia Corporation and Microsoft Corporation. Some factors contributing to its success related to learning environments, but other factors included the focus on entrepreneurship education – which is widely accepted as important including among policy makers – the active use of advocates and the successful management of publicity.

Source: Finland Note, http://www.oecd.org/edu/ceri/implementationandchange.htm.

Another programme, "Culture Path", in Kuopio was included in the earlier round of ILE cases (see OECD, 2013). It is targeted at learners aged 7 to 16 to enhance their social, emotional and physical well-being through culture and art through access to the city's cultural services. This is realised with practical tools for teachers to implement goal-oriented cultural education, and by strengthening co-operation with cultural institutions. The programme is divided into nine "paths" related to art, libraries, theatre, etc., which are designed for the needs and curriculum objectives of a particular grade level, within and across different subjects. Learners visit at least one local cultural institution outside the school environment every year.

A distinguishing feature of the New Zealand LCN strategy is the deliberate positioning of students at the forefront of the network activity with teachers and families closely involved. This in particular brings in students who are Māori, Pasifiika or have special educational needs and whose achievement has not reached national standards. Also involved are the students' families/whānau and teaching professionals who discuss how to move learners along the continuum from passive to active, which often calls for reconsideration of the nature of professional authority in the facilitation of students' learning. Some networks are engaging students and families as co-investigators in the readjustment process while others are more cautious with teachers and leaders still firmly at the forefront. Priority students and their families/whānau are inherently capable, and as agents of their own cultures, are articulate in sharing with teachers and leaders their knowledge about the way they learn and what they may need to change.

In Thuringia (Germany), the start-up project "Development of Innovative Learning Environments" recognises that since education is accomplished not only in formal contexts, the understanding of innovative learning environments goes well beyond educational institutions. It also opens up to family (parents and legal guardians), the wider natural environment, and the larger community and regional environment. There is a close co-operation with the Thuringian initiative "nelecom" (new learning culture in communes).

In British Columbia, the three strategies submitted to OECD/ILE have sought to create a "third space" that is not dominated by provincial or local politics, while receiving some financial support from the government. It is a grass-roots professional initiative, regulated by leadership at the meso level. At the same time, the strong emphasis on Aboriginal education has meant the close working with families and communities and those institutions that represent them. It is thus in both ii) and iii) above.

Much more needs to be said about the nature of spread from formal to non-formal and informal in horizontal meso-level arrangements, but that lies beyond the scope of this report. As regards analysis of the case initiatives, this section has concentrated largely on identifying mixes and partners found in the featured networked initiatives. At a more abstract level, the discussion shows different categories of membership in meso groupings: formal initiatives that bring schools into clusters; voluntary networks of schools and school-based communities of practice; partnerships at the network level bringing schools to work increasingly with different community bodies and non-formal sources of teaching and learning (including service learning); and the introduction into the learning eco-system of increasing numbers of non-formal initiatives that may not operate through recognisable school institutions at all. Figures 5.1a and 5.1b in the next chapter offer a framework for locating these different dimensions of formal/non-formal and vertical/horizontal into a graphical representation of the learning system.

Diffusion and spread through the initiatives

The featured strategies rely on different methods to diffuse innovation. Many such methods may be found in the single "On the Move" programme in Finland. Networking and sharing information, as well as the national and regional seminars, are primary channels. The national programme framework has promoted networking to enable peer learning. Good practices are shared through seminars, brochures and the "On the Move" website. Some of the projects have specific initiatives related to in-service teacher education (e.g. Turku schools are co-operating with the local university teacher education department). The communication strategy includes the website, Facebook pages, newsletters and publications. Media visibility is also an important part of the strategy, and it has been well covered in national, regional and local media, both in printed media and on TV and radio.

Networked activity is, as the title of the strategy suggests, a central part of the New Zealand Learning and Change Network (LCN) programme. The frame illustrated graphically below (Figure 4.2) was designed to initiate networking within and across schools and communities. Network leaders meet together with the facilitator and ministry advisor to frame an activity, before going back to their respective schools to complete the task with students, teachers, families/whānau and leaders. They share and analyse their thinking through across-school visits (virtual or face-to-face). They are then informed and ready to come back together as a network leadership group. This is not seen as constituting network activity per se, but as serving a framing function to co-ordinate network activity, which is within and between the schools and communities. As outlined in the New Zealand System Report: "a good test of healthy networking is to check whether the students, teachers and families/whānau can articulate with ease what it is all about."

Network-to-network learning and change inter alia enhances connectivity. That type of networking has been activated via a series of one-day regional networking sessions held once per term (four times a year), in the five regions within which LCNs are operating. These are for groups of four to eight core network leaders, and serve to:

- give time to reflect on the developments within their own network
- foster reciprocal learning with leaders from other networks
- introduce external experts sharing knowledge relevant to the change priorities
- allow strategy leaders to discuss new elements and/or alterations to the strategy.

Figure 4.2. **The LCN network activity system**

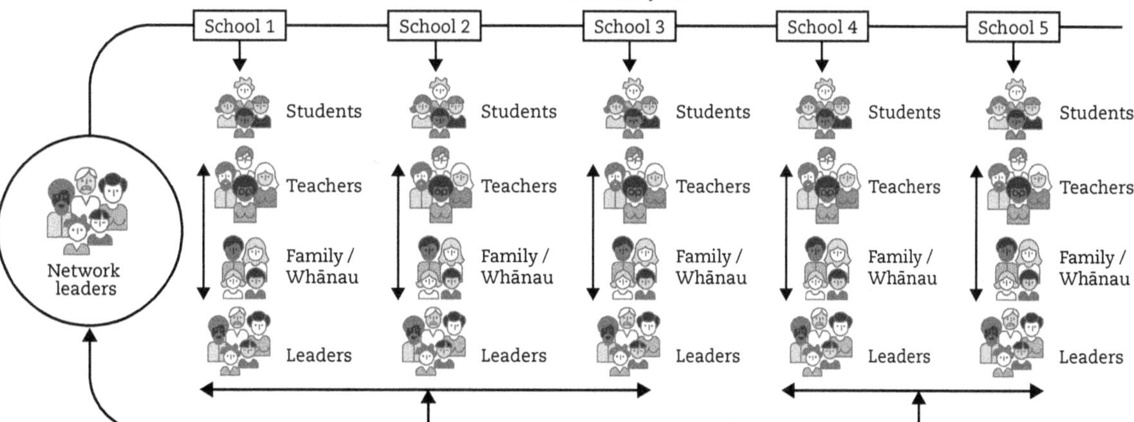

Source: New Zealand Notes, http://www.oecd.org/edu/ceri/implementationandchange.htm.

There is a general LCN website, the ministry has activated an LCN virtual learning network, and some networks are also establishing their own websites. Many are active users of social media to collaborate in creating new knowledge or to spread ideas. Much of the communication at the start was done face-to-face in network leader meetings or via emails but digital communications have increased over time. Similarly, in the Austrian *Lerndesigner* example, both the platform and the portal have grown so rapidly that they became difficult to manage and navigate such that they have to be redesigned and expanded. The South Australian innovation website visits have also been progressively increasing since 2012. Despite the website limitations, "hits" quadrupled throughout 2012 as conferences, workshops, innovation expert events and the national Biennial Forum were underway; the average daily website visits during 2013-14 doubled from those of 2012.

In South Australia, the focus was on the emerging innovation sites, practitioner researchers, and more established innovation schools spreading the innovation message. It has been about contributing towards building the shared culture through the exploring visits to each other's innovations and through the extended networking. Much of the co-ordinated systems work has operated through the department's Innovation Community of Practice involving about 30-45 people from among the 15 initially identified innovation sites and also from innovation site representatives who became part of the community later. Many participants have regularly attended face-to-face events held once each term: to share practice, information and ideas; to highlight emerging issues or opportunities; to discuss new research and papers; and to collaborate in future planning. The Community of Practice has also provided advice for wider dissemination and systems uptake.

Hence, even with a small set of examples the concept of "networking" as if it were a single phenomenon is almost meaningless: it covers a very wide range of practices and groupings, which may or may not be learning focused, may or may not be innovative, may or may not be effective. As the New Zealand example illustrates, networking may be operating at quite different levels simultaneously, including through networking activities. Dynamics may be diverse and not always straightforward, which come is normal in organic and complex eco-systems. The Austrian case study also points to "networks within networks" with varied levels of engagement. It views the *Lerndesigner* Network as a series of different communities of practice, often established through generation-specific experiences among those in each cohort in the qualification programme (each year there is a new "generation" of *Lerndesigners*). The *Lerndesigner* Network is also an online community, though with only a relatively small number of *Lerndesigners* actively participating and thus leading activities. A larger number participate passively through reading posts and downloading materials and forum contributions.

From the examples submitted to OECD/ILE, there are specific further diffusion methods to note. One is the use of especially powerful or innovative sites to serve as beacons in clusters or as system leaders. Another is the use of qualifications to develop expertise in general and a community of expert practice in particular. The third is the role played by regular (often annual) high-profile seminars/conferences as the motor of communication and the means to strengthen the networks and communities of practice.

Cluster leaders/beacons

"Diffusion centres" have been created by the Israeli Ministry for experimental schools to diffuse their innovative models to other schools in Israel. The diffusion centre in-house allows the principal to empower the most dynamic teachers and to enrich their role by becoming the innovation's ambassadors. This team of teachers also brings back ideas from their encounters with others, and in turn enriches creative dialogue within the school. Developing a network of subsidiary diffusion centres thus makes connections across sites but also enhances the robustness of the innovation site itself. Diffusion is further promoted when a school/diffusion centre co-operates with teacher education colleges to provide prospective teachers with practicum and observation opportunities of innovation in action.

The ministry supports this and makes its own contribution to diffusion through complementary work around: encouraging R&D of innovative educational initiatives; examining proposals and requests for experimentation; monitoring the training and assimilation of innovation in educational institutions; encouraging documentation and management of the knowledge accumulated in the course of the experiment; and disseminating the experiment's products throughout the education system.

The English Whole Education Network has three categories of membership for schools, with a small number of leading or "Partner Schools" who help steer the organisation and provide capacity to support the delivery of its services. They are now making a significant contribution to wider system leadership by supporting other schools and leading Teaching School Alliances.

In Thuringia a special feature of the innovation project is the collaboration with start-up project schools that already do exemplary work as innovative learning environments. All participating schools are continuously supported and are encouraged to interconnect with other schools and other institutions. Active support is provided particularly by counsellors for school development, and by several participants and institutions. Exchange, work shadowing and access to multiple information and work material (e.g. on the platform "Thuringian School Portal") are likewise included in the offer.

Specific qualifications

Qualifications are a core feature of the *Lerndesigners* programme in Austria. *Lerndesigners* attend a two-year national qualification programme, which enables them to gain theoretical and practical insights in the six areas of the NMS-House, to develop with one another the knowledge and skills necessary for them to be effective in their own schools as teachers and teacher leaders, and to network with other *Lerndesigners*. The CIEL programme in British Columbia is a year-long graduate programme for formal and informal leaders interested in transforming their schools to higher levels of quality and equity through inquiry and innovative practice. A key aspect of the CIEL programme is that graduates have the opportunity to continue to extend their learning and deepen their connections upon completion through on-going involvement in the Networks of Inquiry and Innovation. In both cases, considerable thought has gone into giving system recognition to innovation through qualifications, into the nature of knowledge that should be diffused through the programme, and into the creation of networks of lead innovators via the shared experience of the learning programme.

Key events

An annual high-profile event is a feature of the British Columbia Networks and the Whole Education Network in England. The "*lernateliers*" are important workshop events organised as part of the Austrian innovation programme. The "Coopère!" and the "Copilote!" are features of the *Décolâge!* initiative, with system-wide seminars for sharing information about design and self-regulated pedagogical leadership practices, as well as their more conventional networking. They serve a variety of purposes: to cement engagement; to strengthen shared norms; to provide but also to share leadership, for professional learning; and to diffuse knowledge, as well as to act as the catalyst for new knowledge. They may also be events for bringing in outside influences to help reinvigorate and regenerate the strategy on a regular basis in ways that are highly visible to all participants.

The ILE framework exemplified in strategy operationalisation

Thus far in this chapter, we have looked at how the different strategies grow the meso level of learning systems and diffuse innovation among the target groups. To do this, we extended the 7+3 framework by incorporating different features of networking that correspond to the questions: Why? Who? and How? One way to bring these together is to use the original ILE framework to ask how well the initiatives are applying it to themselves: how are these strategies themselves applying the lessons of learning principles, designing and redesigning on the basis of learning evidence, and bringing in different partners in their operationalisation.

One of the strongest illustrations of the ILE framework in operation through the strategy is found in the French Community of Belgium's *Décolâge!*. This has followed a set of processes and rationales that resemble the ILE framework in being built around five interconnected "logics":

- a *collaborative management* logic between the different institutional partners of the educative system, so incorporating active learning leadership
- the *development of resources based on scientific contents* logic, so it is research-based
- a logic of *networking and the stimulation of communities of practice* between different educators and teams
- a logic of support for *self-regulated processes of pedagogical conception and leadership* by the networks and organisations, so innovating pedagogical cores
- an *evaluation and feedback logic*, which mirrors the design/evaluation/redesign cycle in the ILE framework.

Learning research was seen as the essential starting point in the Baden-Württemberg *Gemeinschaftsschule* programme just as this was the starting point for the OECD/ILE project. Experts from different educational disciplines clarified research messages on how children of all abilities can learn together and what difficulties a school might have to overcome. As with the learning principles identified through ILE's *The Nature of Learning*, this was intended to provide everybody involved – especially those in the schools themselves – with reliable reference points on the pedagogical and organisational tasks implied by the introduction of this new type of school. Having developed guiding principles, the Baden-Württemberg programme surveyed school change to evaluate the results of the adjustments made by schools based on their self-evaluations. These included:

- recalibrating the learning packages and other materials so that they adapt better to students' individual needs
- strengthening the coaching system, e.g. by putting in more resources or by specifically training teachers for this function
- providing possibilities for in-service training for teachers, e.g. to use co-operative learning approaches
- initiating changes to school building conducive to personalised and co-operative learning, e.g. constructing a learning studio or upgrading classroom equipment
- forming teams of teachers to work on certain aspects of quality improvement together to reduce the workload on the individual teacher.

So the programme has used reviews of reviews to inform further policy and redesign, and it has recognised the need to innovate the pedagogical core and to engage in significant professional learning.

The Slovenian School Development initiative, like the ILE project, began with the principles but then complemented this by a focus on leadership requirements and implementation. They have identified the most distinctive feature of their new approach to be that it was not prepared centrally and then required of all schools invited to take part. The realisation had grown that design should be put in the hands of schools themselves if they are to develop ownership of the innovations. The most important transforming idea of this project was therefore to invite teachers to co-design the project and even more for them to become the leaders of the design process, with central support.

The framework that structures the Austrian NMS *Lerndesigner* initiative in Austria has echoes with the ILE framework both in the principles and in the design applications. The qualification programme for *Lerndesigners* in Austria focuses on equity and excellence in curriculum and instructional development and comprises six development areas. These are deemed essential for fostering change in the learning culture, to be realised by each teacher in each subject in each lesson of the NMS: mindfulness of learning; difference and diversity; competence orientation; "backwards design" curriculum development; differentiated instruction; and assessment. These development areas are represented in the so-called "NMS-House" (see Westfall-Greiter, 2013).

In the Thuringian initiative to grow innovative learning environments and in the context of communal network management, the schools are supported by using training measures designed for the development of innovative learning environments. How this is done mirrors many of the principles and guidelines embodied in the ILE framework.

- *Customisation:* The offers for further training are based on the learner's needs (as well as those of the teachers, the school management and other members of the educational staff) and provide different choices and co-determination.
- *Ownership:* The learners are included into the planning and execution process of the measures and are supported in their role as active propagators, while teachers participating in innovative processes are thereby seen as more likely to implement them as well.
- *Networking:* Co-operation and exchange between the schools, the project management and other project partners encourage the formation of learning and professional communities.
- *Reflection:* This includes analysis, discussion and reflection of educational actions, with self-observation through diaries and portfolios.
- *Practical relevance:* This is a vital element for further training, in order to open up possibilities for active learning.
- *Evaluation:* This includes continuous evaluation and feedback from different project partners during the entire process.

The design and focus of the British Columbia leadership programme (CIEL – the Certificate in Innovative Educational Leadership at Vancouver Island University) also finds parallels with the ILE approach. The emphasis on understanding and application of the spiral of inquiry to change learning outcomes for learners in a range of settings is parallel to the formative design/redesign cycle of the ILE framework. CIEL requires the exploration, analysis and application of the innovative learning environment cases identified in strand two of the ILE project. And there is the expectation that CIEL participants become knowledgeable about the seven learning principles identified in *The Nature of Learning* and the research substantiating these principles.

Main summary highlights

- The initiatives and strategies submitted to the ILE project are *populating the meso level* of their broader eco-systems of learning by creating different networks, chains and communities to lead and diffuse innovation. They offer inspiring examples with the hope of shifting dominant cultures and policy assumptions.
- The submitted initiatives and strategies are *not* "best practices" but they are intended to inspire and show possibilities and problems. They also help extend to analytical frameworks and understanding in the search for growing and sustaining innovative learning.

- Networks, communities of practice and strategies are *constantly emerging, evolving and disappearing*. Overall growth therefore depends on the emergence of new learning-focused networked initiatives outstripping the inevitable decline or disappearance of others.

- Analysis of networked initiatives and strategies can usefully ask how *learning focused* they are; how *horizontally spread* to include the non-formal; and how they *diffuse knowledge, ideas and practice*. These questions have provided the foci for this chapter.

- On the extent of learning focus, the strategies and initiatives submitted to the ILE study are not typical as they are already skewed towards innovative learning. Several of them stand out in the importance given to scanning and identifying the learning challenge at the outset, rather than this being taken as known, and the role played by *learners and their families* in this process.

- Many of the initiatives adopt *variants around 21st century competences* to define their learning aims. But some also emphasise respect and knowledge of cultural values – innovation does not always mean something new but it may be needed to ensure that traditional knowledge and values are not lost.

- *Different mixes* of formal and non-formal may be found. At one end of the spectrum there are the clusters of schools that are required to come together, while less formal is when different schools or communities of practice connect in voluntary ways. Schools may join with different community bodies and interests. There may be purely non-formal bodies or initiatives not operating through school institutions at all.

- In how the strategies and initiatives *connect and diffuse innovation the featured strategies rely on a wide variety of different methods*. The concept of "networking" covers such a wide range of practices and forms that it is largely meaningless to treat it as if it were a single phenomenon. One problem that may be encountered is when a networked initiative becomes a "victim of its own success" and the desired volume of exchange outstrips capacity.

References

Hargreaves, D. (2003), *Education Epidemic: Transforming Secondary Schools through Innovation Networks*, Demos, London.

McGregor, C. (2013), *Aboriginal Inquiry: Lifting ALL Learners: An Impact Assessment of the Aboriginal Enhancement Schools Network (AESN)*, http://inquiry.noii.ca/ (accessed 13/07/2015).

OECD (2013), *Leadership for 21st Century Learning*, Educational Research and Innovation, OECD Publishing, Paris, http://dx.doi.org/10.1787/9789264205406-en.

Owen, S. (2012), "'Fertile Questions', 'Multi-age Groupings', 'Campfires' and 'Master Classes' for specialist skill building: Innovative learning environments and supporting professional learning for 'Teacher Engagers' within South Australian and international contexts", Paper presented at the Joint AARE/APERA Conference, Sydney, http://www.aare.edu.au/data/publications/2012/Owen12.pdf (accessed 16/07/2015).

Tubin, D. (2013), "Learning leadership for innovation at the system level: Israel", in *Leadership for 21st Century Learning*, OECD Publishing, Paris, pp. 170-175, http://dx.doi.org/10.1787/9789264205406-7-en.

Westfall-Greiter, T. (2013), "A network of change agents: Lerndesigners as teacher leaders in Austria", in *Leadership for 21st Century Learning*, OECD Publishing, Paris, pp. 137-145, http://dx.doi.org/10.1787/9789264205406-7-en.

Chapter 5

Transformation and leadership in complex learning systems

Growing and sustaining innovative learning at scale needs to be located in an understanding of the complexity of contemporary learning systems with many settings, players and connections. The creation of flourishing sets of "meso" networked systems is a principal means through which the broader "meta" transformation can take place. Given the importance of relationships and connectors, knowledge is critical to the innovation process and system architecture. Evaluative knowledge is an integral aspect of innovation and implementation. Theories of change are needed to connect actions, strategies and policies with the intended beneficial results, and associated narratives can play an important role. The issue of leadership in such complex systems is fundamental, and increasingly challenging. Often leadership will come from new players. But government leadership remains critical regarding the structure and distribution of learning opportunities, and overseeing coherence of aims, infrastructure and accountability. Government has a privileged role in: i) regulating; ii) incentivising; and iii) accelerating.

This report has positioned innovation and learning environments in wider learning eco-systems. The growing complexity and interdependence of modern societies, closely related to the exponential penetration of digital and other technologies into every dimension of contemporary life, is mirrored in the emergent systems for learning. The complexity of contemporary conditions and systems was addressed in a recent OECD/CERI working paper on governance:

> The complex nature of educational governance, involving myriad layers and actors, can be an overwhelming problem with no clear entry point for policy makers. Traditional approaches, which often focus on questions of top-down versus bottom-up initiatives or levels of decentralisation, are too narrow to effectively address the rapidly evolving and sprawling ecosystems that are modern educational systems. (Snyder, 2013: 6)

At the core of the learning systems for young people are schools and the systems that bind them together. But these are interwoven with a rich and growing set of alternative forms of teaching and learning. Sometimes the formal and the non-formal combine in complex hybrids. Even within formal schooling, there are countless networks and connections that spread well outside designated roles and relationships as educators come together in voluntary networks and communities of practice. Growing and sustaining innovative learning at scale needs to be located in understanding this complexity. There are many settings for learning in the topography of contemporary systems, and framing that wider system permits consideration of how the core of formal schooling relates with the wider eco-system so as to optimise its own contribution.

Complexity should not mean chaos, therefore, and it puts additional premium on developing frameworks which might usefully inform the activities of the many players in educational innovation, whether from the policy or the practice side. This chapter begins by considering architecture for the meta level. This distinguishes the importance of the meso level and of network connectedness. As we move away from seeing the larger system as a unified formal entity, with a single institutional structure and policy and governance authority, system change critically takes place through the myriad meso-level initiatives, networks and communities of practice, some large-scale, some small. Many may affect no more than relatively small numbers of learners and communities but taken together, their effect can be profound.

Privileging networks at once raises the question of what the connections are in complex eco-systems that bind people and organisations together. This chapter privileges the role of knowledge in offering connection and "glue", and therefore too the role of evaluation and prototyping. There follows more detailed discussion of change and leadership, drawing again on examples from the submitted strategy cases. The chapter discusses theories of change and narratives, and concludes with discussion of the particular role of government policy.

Transforming the meta system via the meso level

The meta level can be understood as the aggregation of smaller meso- and environment-level systems together with the architecture, culture and context that they share. Given that meta boundaries may be drawn widely or narrowly there is no single definition of what it encompasses though the formal school system, within its national or regional boundaries, is clearly an important core structure in terms of setting rules, expectations, conditions, resources and so forth.

At the meso level, some of the relevant providers and networks are outside the formal structures and settings, though many will include formal school partners and participants. There are many signs that this diversification is taking place, in part driven by demand and in part by the possibilities opened up by the power of technology to make connections. This is seen in the United States for instance:

> [The] change involves the development and proliferation of design-based networks of schools, both charter and not, operating within and sometimes across communities – for example, Urban Assembly schools in New York, High Tech High schools in San Diego, Green Dot schools and Aspire schools in Los Angeles, and KIPP schools, Expeditionary Learning schools, and Big Picture schools in many places. These networks challenge the traditional conception of the school district as the key shaper of a school's mission, culture, instructional design, and curriculum. Some of these school design networks also challenge what was once a sharp distinction between in-school and out-of-school by means of their use of community settings and online formats for teaching and learning. (McDonald, 2014: 140)

Similarly, Jackson and Petersen (2015) describe networked arrangements as emerging learning eco-systems around four different models:

- school chains, which are groups of schools sharing a mission and acting as a micro system
- locally embedded hubs, responding through innovation to particular needs in a community or locality
- innovation zones, centrally facilitated innovation strategies in, for example, a city creating a network of schools, system leaders and broader education partners
- looser networks and coalitions, socialising new ways of working among professionals and school leaders.

Together, these are seen to have clear advantages through bringing in outside influences, creating economies of scale and more diverse "footprints of practice", and facilitating transfer. Each may have particular advantages and drawbacks, as in their view:

> Hubs and iZones can more effectively bring into practice strong, new approaches, or incubate the adaptation of effective approaches from other systems. Past experience indicates that hubs and iZones have limitations when it comes to scaling effective practice beyond the initial group of schools. Chains and franchises have been most effective at spreading consistent practice across schools, but their separateness from the wider system can negatively impact wider influence. Looser networks and coalitions have been effective in socialising spreading new practice across a whole system but their looser nature impacts their sustainability prospects. (Jackson and Petersen, 2015: 4).

These changes become much more significant when, as McDonald suggests, they are seen as a heavy trend rather than isolated examples to be understood one-by-one in isolation. Therefore, the argument goes further than defining the meta level through its constituent learning environments and networks through seeing in the creation of flourishing sets of meso networked learning eco-systems the means through which the broader meta transformation can take place. This is clearly different from focusing on the "middle" level within the formal school structure: while it may be compatible with the notion of "leading from the middle" (Fullan, 2005), it is distinct from it in being cast in terms of wider learning eco-systems (though not ignoring formal policy and governance, see below).

Visualising more connected, diverse meta systems

Figure 5.1a. **A weakly-connected meta system**

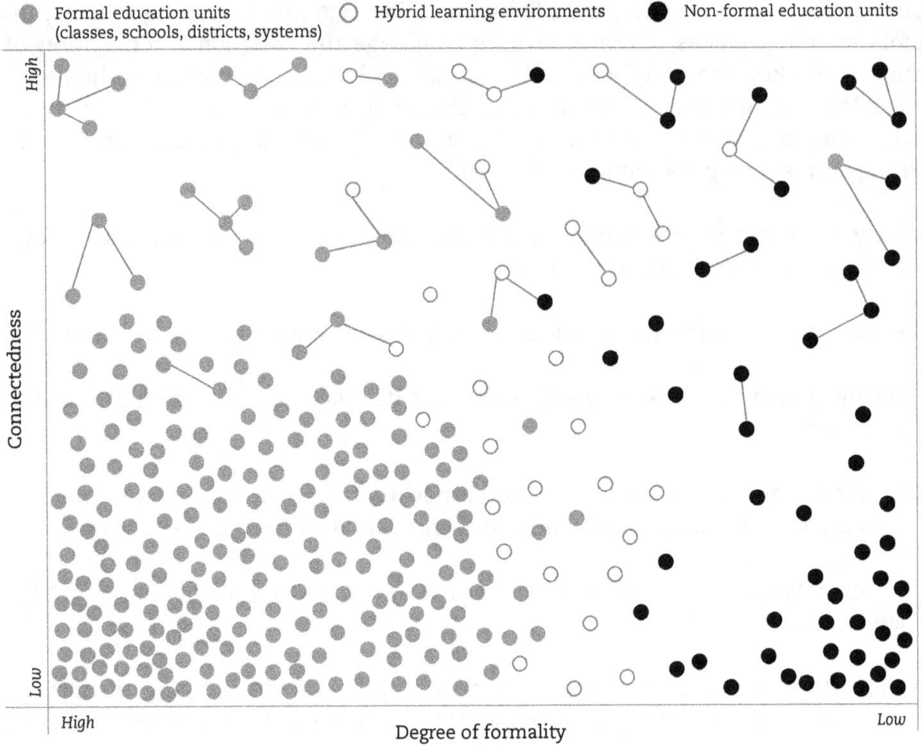

Figure 5.1b. **A networked meta system**

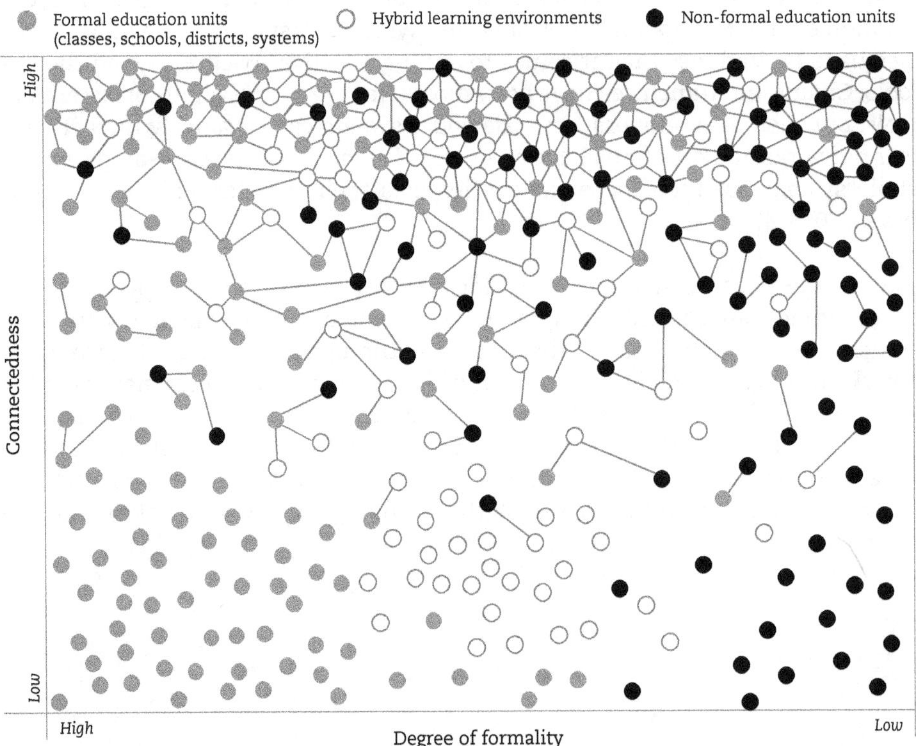

Figures 5.1a and 5.1b represent the meta system, including formal, non-formal and hybrid forms, and units of education. Moving up the space, there are more connections of formal units, which can be clusters and chains of schools. Moving across, more of them are connected among themselves or connected with partners as hybrids or from the non-formal sector. The hybrids are combining, for instance, work and learning, sports and learning, community service and formal learning. On the right are non-formal educational providers.

Figure 5.1a represents a hypothetical weakly-networked meta learning system. There are few networks and cross-school communities, there is very little evidence of hybrids, and while there are some non-formal programmes and providers as these respond to demand to alternatives to schools there is little connection between them and the formal system. The networked learning system (Figure 5.1b) implies a significant increase in the number of groups, organisations and organisms devoted to learning as units not only work by themselves as before but connect up to a flourishing range of collaborative groupings. The networked system shows the learning space is fuller horizontally. There are more non-formal providers and programmes too, encouraged by the dynamism of learning and the opportunities opened up by technology and by demand; some of these form networks totally outside the formal system. But often, the formal and the non-formal come together, and fill the "hybrid" space in the middle. There are more networks and communities of practice created in the formal system as it encourages clusters, networks and collaboration among districts, schools, classes and teachers as well.

The dynamics of learning innovation and change

Learning eco-systems constantly change, with groupings forming and disbanding all the time; as organic, they are less predictable. In being less defined by acquired position and regulated status, they rely critically on relationships and connectivity whose importance grows. Especially important are knowledge and ideas as connectors. Increasingly, but not exclusively, they depend on communication technologies. The BC study refers to Manuel Castells (2000) in distinguishing between the "space of place" and a "space of flows". The former refers to where peoples' experiences and activities actually take place and the latter is about the ways in which ideas move from one place to another.

Networks and knowledge

Networks can be singled out, not because they are by themselves always effective or innovative but because they offer the connectors through which knowledge passes and ultimately collaborative action takes place. Suggett (2014) summarises how, in very different policy areas, networks are seen as pivotal to rapid change and securing key breakthroughs: "they have proliferated to an astonishing extent within different countries, policy areas and levels of governance (Sorensen and Torfing, 2009: 235)". They are particularly valued for their capacity to bring diverse perspectives to the table, whether from inside or outside government, clarify problems, facilitate co-ordination and actually implement change.

Effective networks can cut through complex hierarchies and generate new solutions to intractable and often challenging local problems whether in preventative health, welfare issues such as social housing and support for vulnerable youth, energy solutions, the environment, or in restructuring regional economies (Bourgon, 2011). Complex issues put a premium on the capacity of leaders and organisations to take account of a multitude of interdependencies and work across traditional boundaries. Well-functioning collaborative networks add high value and can enable the whole to become more than the sum of its parts.

Box 5.1. **WMR reform, Victoria (Australia)**

The WMR reform was a systemic intervention strategy, designed to galvanise a collective effort to lift performance. The strategy aimed to improve the learning outcomes and well-being of all government school students in the region (including those performing well) by developing the instructional knowledge and practices of teachers, school leaders and regional staff. The focus was on literacy and numeracy as the "building blocks for access to a rich curriculum and successful transition pathways", and was subsequently extended to other areas of the curriculum.

The region had divided its schools into 7 networks, each comprised around 20 schools and those schools and the associated regional support infrastructure were the organisational centre points for the region's strategy. The approach to system-wide improvement was generated through co-design and mutual commitment between the region and all schools. This process enabled the region and its schools to establish powerful overarching goals, a common language, and an interlocking set of mutual expectations and actions. They chose a proven instructional model for literacy and numeracy improvement that had an excellent track record through which expert consultants and coaches could continuously build teacher capacity. That methodology was extended to other areas of the curriculum as the strategy progressed.

Four principles guided the improvement strategy:

i) *Collective efficacy:* This occurs when teachers collectively believe all students can learn and achieve. It is a lead indicator of the potential for growth in student learning.

ii) *Focus on the "instructional core":* The only place to improve student outcomes is in the classroom; that requires focusing on the relationships between student, teacher and content.

iii) *Layered learning:* This is about continuous capacity building that emphasises that everyone learns together about the same things.

iv) *Gradual release of responsibility:* This is a theory of learning that moves the learner from teacher–directed instruction to student-centred collaboration and independent practice. It is applicable to all learning including students in the classroom and professional learning for teachers and principals.

These principles were underpinned by "de-privatised" classrooms, where professional practices are developed and refined through openness and collaboration. The strategy progressed through four broad interlocking stages.

- setting the challenge and building the shared purpose
- early implementation: establishing role clarity and tight webs of reciprocal responsibilities
- relentless implementation: changing what schools do, particularly instruction for literacy and numeracy
- emerging collective efficacy: flourishing innovation and network learning.

Source: Victoria (Australia) Note, http://www.oecd.org/edu/ceri/implementationandchange.htm.

Knowledge to connect, for design, as implementation

Given the importance of relationships and connectors, knowledge is a critical part of the dynamics of the innovation process and learning architecture. In OECD/CERI work on systemic innovation, it has been accorded a pivotal status in the developed frameworks (OECD, 2009):

> *The central role of knowledge*[...] the knowledge base lies at the heart of the process of innovation, with each stage feeding into the knowledge base and the knowledge base providing input into each stage[...] The concept of knowledge is defined here in its broadest possible sense and includes knowledge arising from a variety of sources (*e.g.* academic research, field practice) and of various types including explicit and tacit knowledge. (OECD, 2009: 94, 178)

It has also been accorded a central role in OECD/CERI work on the governance of complex education systems, on the argument that:

> Knowledge is crucial for governance and governance is indispensable for knowledge creation and dissemination. As complexity in education systems continues to increase, governance systems' capacity to learn becomes more and more crucial. Most institutions involved in educational policy have become knowledge-intensive organisations whose success depends most critically on their ability to learn. (Fazekas and Burns, 2012: 23)

Within ILE, Earl and Timperley (2015) refer to "evaluative thinking", which privileges actionable knowledge in the implementation process. Earl and Timperley argue that evaluative thinking is a necessary component of successful innovation and involves more than measurement and quantification. Combining evaluation with innovation requires discipline in the innovation and flexibility in the evaluation. The knowledge bases for both innovation and evaluation have advanced dramatically in recent years in ways that have allowed synergies to develop between them; the different stakeholders can bring evaluative thinking into innovation in ways that capitalise on these synergies.

Evaluative thinking contributes to new learning by providing evidence to chronicle, map and monitor the progress, successes, failures and roadblocks in the innovation as it unfolds. It involves thinking about what evidence will be useful during the course of the innovation activities, establishing the range of objectives and targets that make sense to determine their progress, and building knowledge and developing practical uses for the new information, throughout the trajectory of the innovation. Having a continuous cycle of generating hypotheses, collecting evidence, and reflecting on progress, allows the stakeholders (e.g. innovation leaders, policy makers, funders, participants in innovation) an opportunity to try things, experiment, make mistakes and consider where they are, what went right and what went wrong, through a fresh review of the course and the effects of the innovation.

In this way evaluative knowledge is not something apart from the innovation and change process that comes along afterwards to assess impact. It is an integral aspect of innovation and implementation. Participants are empowered to take informed leadership decisions and to engage in design precisely because evaluative thinking and activity is a constant part of the process. It is thus formative, and gives all participants, partners and leadership stakeholders a common language and evidence base on which shared designs and projects can be built.

Theories of change

Michael Fullan (2007: 14) notes that many change attempts fail because "no distinction is made between theories of change (what causes change) and theories of changing (how to influence those causes)". It is not just about having a robust theory of change but also a theory of how to change the things highlighted by the initial change theory, and the means to be able to do so. In learning eco-systems and in education in general, these cannot be guaranteed as so much lies beyond the gift of governments. Fullan later describes (2011) many of the traditional reform instruments as the "wrong drivers" – accountability pressures, individual teacher and leadership quality approaches, technology, and fragmented strategies – because they do not lead to culture change and re-professionalisation, and often de-motivate. Instead, in his view, the "right" drivers include the focus on the learning-teaching-assessment nexus, social capital to build the profession, pedagogy matching technology, and developing systemic synergies.

The strategies and initiatives submitted to the ILE study exhibit diverse theories of change. The ministry's model of change in the Israeli experimental school policy is that it begins in schools, operating within an agreed framework for developing innovative design, and is then implemented and spread to additional schools. This model is based on three assumptions. First, there are many initiatives all over the educational system that need backing and a shield, which the ministry should provide. Second, for an educational initiative to become an innovative learning environment, it needs five years of support to provide schools with time, structure and training in order to experiment and elaborate the educational initiative. Third, after five years, in schools that have shown themselves to be successful ILEs, there is a need to establish a diffusion centre whose responsibility is to share the know-how with other interested schools.

The theory of action in the Victoria example has been that local level leadership in clusters of approximately 20 schools within a geographic area would:

- locate accountability for improvement where it matters at the regional and network level
- allow nominated network leaders collectively to build deep knowledge of the needs of schools within their clusters so as to support their improvement agenda
- ensure that local allocation of resourcing and provision decisions made a good match to the collective interests of the community served by each network of schools
- provide sufficient resources dedicated to school improvement to lead to improvement in the performance of all schools within the Victorian government system.

In New Zealand, LCN strategy leaders have learned a great deal about how to activate lateral networking. A shift has taken place from central monopolisation of expertise and authority towards more shared approaches to theory development. It has been a shift from a few strategy leaders visioning and theorising to LCN participants growing their own images of future-focused learning environments and articulating their underlying theories. This has privileged learning and process so that spread is about influencing mind-set and practice shifts among educators operating in groups of their choice.

The change strategy for the linked innovation and inquiry networks in British Columbia has five key dimensions:

Find the deviance: Using a "find the positive deviance" inquiry model, innovative practices, and regular presentations and online publications of case studies of inquiry/innovation keep the flow of promising possibilities alive.

Link the influencers: In peer-to-peer networks the most powerful influencers tend to be those who have the strongest repertoires of changed practice combined with a spirit of curiosity. It is important that as many roles as possible are linked – the linkage involving social media, annual symposia, widespread use of video, focused social events, research studies, readings, and face-to-face meetings for network leaders.

Infuse intelligence: There is need for a shared and open-ended framework to provide a disciplined approach and to encourage coherence across large geographic and institutional spaces.

Develop fresh energy: There is need to infuse regular, high-level doses of fresh energy to keep the culture growing and vital (especially, in their case, via the Center for Innovative Leadership Development at Vancouver Island University).

Persist: Persistence is key, and the evolution from strong to innovative requires cultivation. Persistence matters in the building of networks and in accomplishing difficult goals through sustained effort and imagination.

For KwaZulu-Natal in South Africa a simple programme theory is seen as providing the first step.

Box 5.2. **KwaZulu-Natal ICT implementation programme theory (South Africa)**

IF learners experiencing barriers to learning are identified and given access to appropriate support by trained teachers and appropriate structures within and outside the school, **THEN** they are more likely to attend school regularly, be more attentive in class and benefit from learning activities.

AND IF teachers have a thorough understanding of the subject content that they teach and are trained in learner-centred approaches to teach using a variety of resources that take into account the diverse learning needs of learners under their care, **THEN** learners will be encouraged to take greater responsibility for their learning by engaging in carefully selected tasks using the relevant resources made available to them.

AND IF schools are equipped with appropriate interactive technology with the necessary digital content, **THEN** learners and teachers will have access to technology-based teaching and learning resources.

AND IF teachers are adequately trained in using the technology to plan and present lessons using learner-centred approaches that encourage learners to use the technology to explore concepts, find relevant information and participate effectively in lessons, **THEN** learners will have greater opportunities to access relevant resources and engage in self-learning activities.

AND IF teachers participate actively in and share their experiences at teacher professional development learning committees, **THEN** they will reflect on their own practice, benefit from shared experiences, and gain confidence in their own content knowledge and innovative teaching skills.

AND IF learners and teachers are supported in establishing classrooms as innovative learning environments through classroom visits by master teachers, **THEN** learners will improve their education achievement.

Source: Victoria (Australia) Note, http://www.oecd.org/edu/ceri/implementationandchange.htm.

Because of the need for shared understandings in complex situations, it is important that the theory of change is not an arcane plan known only to a privileged few in central office. The theory needs to be contextualised and its rationale clear. As more and more are involved in collectively shaping the direction and success of eco-learning systems, they need projects around which to work together. This emphasises the importance of narratives which give different players a sense of direction and express why change itself is important. A narrative must be reasonably succinct so that the important "story" can be told. It builds on a theory of change but is at once more accessible and embracing. It is partly about communication – clear, understandable messages – but it is about much more as the underlying theory and story that feed the messages must be meaningful and ambitious and appropriate for the context.

Time and implementation

Relationships, connections and trust take time to form. The interaction of networks and communities unfold in time, not instantly. It takes time to learn, no matter who is doing the learning – individuals, classes, schools, networks, communities of practice, districts, stakeholders or ministries of education. And with time comes change: change in context and relationships, change in the form of growth, and in the form of decline and disappearance as well.

Growing innovative learning environments organically, based on sound knowledge and professional commitment, clearly cannot be achieved at scale overnight. Several of the featured strategies describe how they were implemented through pilots. The Austrian NMS Reform began in 2008 with 67 pilot schools, before later being mandated and in which system-wide completion is foreseen for 2018. The Teacher Education Programme on Early Numeracy and Literacy in the Former Yugoslav Republic of Macedonia went through a careful review and preparation phase in 2008-09 before full implementation. The New Zealand Learning and Change Network Strategy began in five pilot networks representing 45 schools/kura before spreading to many more. The Thüringen Development of Inclusive and Innovative Learning Environments programme in Germany began in

40 "start-up" schools with the view that they should become reference schools for those who join the programme at a later stage.

These examples represent pilots in a genuine sense. But often the term is used to refer not to genuine leading experiments to be built on over the longer-term but to relatively small-scale initiatives without the serious intention that they will ever lead to wider adoption or change. A common experience is for funded programme innovations to last only for as long as the additional funding is available and for practice to slip back to business as usual once this has dried up. There is the familiar "Hawthorne Effect" whereby the experience of the reference pilots is unrepresentative because the additional spotlight and support which the pilot has received makes it an inaccurate guide to potential adoption by others. Without a commitment to sustain the change, pilots become ends in themselves without larger system relevance.

Strategies for educational innovation and change necessarily take time to put into effect, no matter what the urgency shown. The Swedish "Mother Tongue Theme Site", for instance, started with 4 languages in 2001 and had reached materials in 45 languages and over 10 000 web pages over a decade later. The Slovenian Renovation programme has been put in place through a 10-year process. Even those strategies that reported relatively swift progress – for example, the 2-3 years for the sustained work with networks to show results in British Columbia or the 5 years for the Victorian WMR strategy – can be viewed as slow by the timetables of political cycles.

Box 5.3. **South Australia innovation strategies and objectives**

A three-fold strategy was collaboratively devised in regard to wider systems diffusion:

- a department-coordinated hosted site visits/learning programme was established and promoted
- awards of small practitioner grants to engage and upskill emerging innovation schools in gathering data and evidence about their innovative practices
- an expanded Community of Practice operating through meetings and communicating regularly, with internal and external partnerships continuing to be fostered and impacted.

The systems diffusion approach, building on earlier strategies to disseminate innovation widely across the department, has been to:

- build a systems innovation culture and more innovative practices through establishing a series of hosted site visits/learning programmes which increase understanding of innovative practices and the impacts on student learning and also support interested others to become more innovative in their work
- support emerging innovation sites through small grants and practitioner research skill-building and gathering evidence about this innovative practice and its impact on teachers and leaders
- increase innovation learning through an expanded Community of Practice, with members working together to share issues and disseminate ideas across the department and more widely, including through links established with broader professional, national and international partnerships and networks.

Source: South Australia Notes, http://www.oecd.org/edu/ceri/implementationandchange.htm.

The importance of time is partly a matter of the processes involved in moving beyond the early innovators to reach a critical mass of practitioners. It is also a matter of the phases of learning and implementation that need to be passed through in order to embed the learning strategies in systems and institutions. This is formalised in the New Zealand LCN strategy into four phases of development: (i) establishing infrastructure to operate as a network, (ii) profiling the current learning environment to understand student achievement challenges and agree on change priorities, (iii) implementing a plan to address the change priorities, and (iv) sustaining useful changes and agreeing on next steps. The strategy in Victoria (Australia) to make a significant difference to outcomes in the Western

Metropolitan Region was also designed around four big phases: initiation, early implementation, relentless implementation and deepening learning. Only by reaching the final phase can the benefits of the change fully be seen. This also warns against looking to evaluate programmes early when no time has elapsed for change properly to embed, still less to impact on learning; the results of such evaluations are bound to be disappointing.

The Austrian NMS strategy has explicitly worked in terms of the different "generations" that have passed through the qualification cycles as *Lerndesigners*. Instead of assuming that the already-qualified earlier generations had become active and expert and no longer in need of attention, networking and professional development opportunities were established for them as well in order to keep them engaged in the reform process. It is an impressive example where sustaining as well as creating the change has featured in programme design.

A perennial problem in educational reform is that the timetables involved in making school-level educational change are not matched by the political timetables of government programmes and funding. Rather than build on the foundations laid in a previous administration, the temptation may be to scrap existing initiatives and start afresh. One means of mitigating the obviously negative impact of mismatched political and educational change cycles is to unhitch innovations from close association with particular government programmes. The more that government is only one partner among several, the less vulnerable are programmes to being wound up when administrations or personalities change. The BC innovators refer to this as establishing "third spaces" in the endeavour to create some distance from politically-charged environments into spaces that permit more professional dialogue.

Even so, the dictates of urgent action mean that educators and innovators, and not only elected politicians, want and need to see results quickly. Several of the ILE cases refer to the importance of rapid prototyping, which combines the two dynamic dimensions we have focused on in the learning architecture: knowledge and time. The South Australia case refers to the value of rapid prototyping, taking the argument of a school leader from the innovation Community of Practice that in the innovation culture practitioner research often takes too long and is costly to do well.

Austria similarly identified prototyping as the method for developing virtual Professional Learning Communities (PLC). In this, the challenge was to keep busy teacher leaders connected to an Austria-wide community of practice and to encourage them to participate actively in nationwide development activities. The virtual environment was redesigned to make it more navigable, user-friendly and manageable. There were organisational challenges, including that busy teachers from different schools with different timetables may have difficulty fixing appointments for the virtual meetings. There were technical challenges, too, including in the variable technical resources and digital skills of the different individual participants. The vignettes captured during the prototyping reveal the virtual PLC work as powerful for adult learning.

Complexity and system leadership

The difference between complication and complexity revolves around three criteria: the extent to which the model or system can be designed, predicted, and controlled. (This discussion draws especially on Hannon, 2014.) While a jet engine is immensely complicated, with many moving parts, it scores highly on the degree to which it can be designed, predicted and controlled. At the other end of the spectrum, systems such as cities – while they are to varying degrees designed and susceptible to prediction and control – are nevertheless categorically different. They are characterised by a high degree of interdependence of elements and connectivity. Interaction is critical. Complex systems are more autonomous and more difficult to predict.

In such complex, diverse and challenging contexts, can the processes of change actually be led? We have been accustomed to thinking about system leadership as emanating from the political or governmental bases, or in some exceptional cases from leaders of influential institutions. Now, with the multiplicity of actors and agencies (and funding streams), sources of leadership may be more plentiful, but the task is more complex.

Comprehending something about the dynamics of complex systems is essential to effecting change, and particularly to promoting scale and diffusion of innovative effective approaches. The mobilisation and empowerment of the *demand* side as part of this have still to be fully explored. If more learners and their families understand what powerful personalised learning looks like, they are more likely to demand it and seek it out – and supply may well follow. A number of new players are paying particular attention to the demand side, and exercising leadership through that route, such as foundations.

A further significant shift in the locus of system leadership for the future derives from the globalisation of education. This process has been accelerated by international measures including the OECD Programme for International Student Assessment (PISA) and also by the technologies which are largely borderless, and indeed as many global companies become deeply involved in education. One implication of this globalised context is that system leadership can now be exercised through use of technology globally to showcase and enable transformed environments to influence others. This raises the issue of the distinctive and irreplaceable role of national/jurisdictional governments. Globalisation is likely to further amplify the effect of the new players, including:

- corporations entering the education market in different ways (for example, running low-cost private schools in Asia)
- capital and venture philanthropy operating globally, often on a much greater scale
- technology start-ups innovating learning analytics and the applications of big data to learning contexts
- cultural organisations diversifying to create learning offers
- businesses – more of which are now engaging with schools to create extended internships for school-age learners to diversify and root their learning in real-life contexts.

But, globalisation should not necessarily be conceived of as an innovative forward-looking force. Less visionary reactions will be defensive and backward-looking, seeing the response to the international comparisons such as those furnished through the PISA surveys to lie in a mythologised version of the past in ways that will not serve well the demands of their learners, their societies or their economies.

The role of government policy

The complexity of contemporary learning systems, and the need to engage those most involved in teaching and learning on the ground, mean that top-down mandating is inappropriate and even common policy metaphors such as "levers", "alignment" and "scale-up" are inadequate and excessively mechanistic for the nature of 21st century educational change. Much of the role of policy to make desirable change resides in helping to set conditions and create climates. It is about helping to grow capacities and foster collaboration. It is about encouraging learning-focused networks and communities of practice.

As described in the New Zealand ILE report, many of these grounded efforts have been catalysed by government support and eventually become part of everyday life, though with varying levels of direct ministry involvement. In the French Community of Belgium, the programme Décolâge! has been driven from the office of the Minister of Education, and has sought to introduce meta-level change into a complex school system. Its ILE report argues that the government should develop a new type of management, in which, in addition to its role of defining norms and rules, evaluation, and granting subsidies, it should have a supportive role in translation, innovation and what is called "cre-action".

But alongside creating conducive conditions for innovative learning systems to flourish there is also a clear leadership role to be played as well. Many of the strategies discussed in this report have depended on government design and leadership. Ministries and system agencies provide the legitimacy and the breadth to play a privileged role in this respect. They have the resources and responsibility for schools that make them central to the change process.

The overall structure and distribution of learning opportunities is an area where government has an especially important role to play. This is one of the key tasks of policy, in seeking to generate coherence of aims, infrastructure and accountability. The ILE case strategies suggest a number of ways to work towards greater coherence. One is from Finland, in which the national core curriculum process can draw on the project experiences of innovative learning environments. The core curricula and their related curriculum support materials thereby inform the reform process – at the least they help avoid incoherence and duplication but more positively they reinforce each other. Another example is about ensuring that the innovation uses system-wide standards so as to avoid establishing competing (and confusing) benchmarks (e.g. the British Columbia Networks of Inquiry and Innovation which are grounded in BC standards of performance).

The sister OECD/CERI project to ILE (Governing Complex Education Systems) has similarly looked at the options and strategies available to governments when traditional "hard" forms of governance cease to work or are no longer appropriate. In looking at different models for "soft" central governance it finds some commonalities in them being multi-staged (again emphasising the time factor), and they place particular emphasis on transparency and publicity (knowledge and narratives) while operating through soft sanctions (Wilkoszewski and Sundby, 2014).

Among the strategic options for government action, informed by a sense of how the intended change might actually result in desired outcomes, the following should feature prominently:

Regulate: Identify and mitigate risks; establish quality assurance protocols; manage data, privacy and procurement.

Incentivise: Establish third party brokers and enablers; dedicate resources to establishing partnerships.

Accelerate: Create internal and external enabling environments; measure impact and promote desirable change.

A key will be to facilitate *relationships* between government, schools and players who have expertise, ideas and resources to offer in the ambition to innovate education.

Main summary highlights

- Growing and sustaining innovative learning at scale needs to be located in an understanding of the *complexity of contemporary learning systems* with many settings, players and connections. Framing this broader understanding permits consideration of how the core of formal schooling relates with the wider eco-system so as to optimise its own contribution.

- The creation of flourishing sets of meso networked learning eco-systems is a principal means through which the broader meta transformation can take place. One classification of such networked learning arrangements, in which each has a place in the larger meta system but with its own advantages and drawbacks, is: school chains; locally embedded hubs; innovation zones; and looser networks and coalitions.

- Given the importance of relationships and connectors, *knowledge* is a critical part of the dynamics of the innovation process and learning system architecture.

- As part of this, *evaluative knowledge* is not something apart that comes later to assess impact: it is an integral aspect of innovation and implementation. Participants are empowered to take informed leadership decisions and to engage in design precisely because evaluative thinking and activity is a constant part of the process.

- *Theories of change* are needed to connect actions, strategies and policies with the intended beneficial results. It is not just about addressing what causes change, but how to influence those causes.

- *Narratives* give the different players a sense of direction and reasons why change itself is important. A narrative must be reasonably succinct so that the important "story" can be told; it builds on a theory of change but is at once more accessible and embracing.

- Relationships, connections and trust take *time*; the interaction of networks and communities unfold in time, not instantly; it takes time to learn, no matter who is doing the learning – individuals, classes, schools, networks, communities of practice, districts, stakeholders or ministries of education.

- Several of the featured strategies were implemented through *pilots* giving time to learn about processes before going to larger scale. But, often the term is used to refer to relatively small-scale initiatives without the serious intention that they will ever lead to wider adoption and which last only for as long as the additional funding is available. Some have preferred *rapid prototyping*, working to much shorter time frames.

- The complexity of contemporary learning systems, and the need to engage those most involved in teaching and learning on the ground, mean that *top-down mandating is inappropriate* and even common policy metaphors such as "levers", "alignment" and "scale-up" are inadequate and excessively mechanistic for the nature of 21st century educational change.

- The *issue of leadership in such complex systems* becomes critical, and increasingly challenging. Often leadership will come from new players, outside the traditional system. But government leadership remains vital and its legitimacy, breadth, and the capacity to access resources often make it central to the change process.

- The overall structure and distribution of learning opportunities is an area where *government* has an especially important role to play, in seeking to generate coherence of aims, infrastructure and accountability. Among the strategic options for government action, they are especially well placed for: i) regulating; ii) incentivising; and iii) accelerating.

References

Bourgon, J. (2011), *A New Synthesis of Public Administration: Serving in the 21st century*, McGill-Queens University Press, Canada.

Castells, M. (2000), *The Rise of the Network Society*, Blackwell, Oxford.

Cheng, E.C.K and M.L. Mo (2013), "The approach of Learning Study: its origin and implications", *OECD Education Working Papers*, No. 94, OECD Publishing, Paris, http://dx.doi.org/10.1787/5k3wjp0s959p-en.

Dumont, H., D. Istance, and F. Benavides (2010), *The Nature of Learning: Using Research to Inspire Practice*, Educational Research and Innovation, OECD Publishing, Paris, http://dx.doi.org/10.1787/9789264086487-en.

Earl, L. and Timperley H. (2015), "Evaluative thinking for successful educational innovation", OECD Education Working Papers, No. 122, OECD Publishing, Paris, http://dx.doi.org/ 10.1787/5jrxtk1jtdwf-en.

Fazekas, M. and T. Burns (2012), "Exploring the complex interaction between governance and knowledge in education", *OECD Education Working Papers*, No. 67, OECD Publishing, Paris, http://dx.doi.org/10.1787/5k9flcx2l340-en.

Fullan, M. (2007), *The New Meaning of Educational Change*, Teacher's College Press, New York, NY.

Fullan, M. (2011), *Choosing the Wrong Drivers for Whole System Reform*, Centre for Strategic Education Seminar Series No. 204, Melbourne, Australia.

Hannon, V. (2014), "Innovation, systems and system leadership", http://www.oecd.org/edu/ceri/Hannon%20paper_ILE%20strand%203.pdf (accessed 24/07/2015).

Hargreaves, A. and M. Fullan (2012), *Professional Capital: Transforming Teaching in Every School*, Teachers College Press, London and New York, NY.

Jackson, D. with A. Petersen (2015), "Emerging learning ecosystems: new alliances, new partnerships and new players", London, Innovation Unit, http://gelponline.org/sites/default/files/resource-files/gelp_learning_ecosystems.pdf (accessed 17/07/2015).

McDonald, J.P (2014), *American School Reform: What Works, What Fails, and Why*, The University of Chicago Press, Chicago, IL.

OECD (2013a), *Innovative Learning Environments*, Educational Research and Innovation, OECD Publishing, Paris, http://dx.doi.org/10.1787/9789264203488-en.

OECD (2013b), *Leadership for 21st Century Learning*, Educational Research and Innovation, OECD Publishing, Paris, http://dx.doi.org/10.1787/9789264205406-6-en.

OECD (2013c), *Synergies for Better Learning: An International Perspective on Evaluation and Assessment*, OECD Publishing, Paris, http://dx.doi.org/10.1787/9789264190658-en.

OECD (2009), *Working Out Change: Systemic Innovation in Vocational Education and Training*, Educational Research and Innovation, OECD Publishing, Paris, http://dx.doi.org/10.1787/9789264075924-en.

Snyder, S (2013), "The simple, the complicated, and the complex: educational reform through the lens of complexity theory", *OECD Education Working Papers*, No. 96, OECD Publishing, Paris, http://dx.doi.org/10.1787/5k3txnpt1lnr-en.

Sørensen, E. and Torfing, J. (2009), "Making governance networks effective and democratic through meta-governance", *Public Administration*, 87 (2), pp. 234-58.

Suggett, D. (2014) "Networking as system policy: balancing vertical and horizontal dimensions", http://www.oecd.org/edu/ceri/Suggett%20Networks%20paper%20formatted.pdf (accessed 24/07/2015).

Wilkoszewski, H. and E. Sundby (2014), "Steering from the centre: new modes of governance in multi-level education systems", *OECD Education Working Papers*, No. 109, OECD Publishing, Paris, http://dx.doi.org/10.1787/5jxswcfs4s5g-en.

Zitter, I. and A. Hoeve (2012), "Hybrid learning environments: Merging learning and work processes to facilitate knowledge integration and transitions", *OECD Education Working Papers*, No. 81, OECD Publishing, Paris, http://dx.doi.org/10.1787/5k97785xwdvf-en.

ORGANISATION FOR ECONOMIC CO-OPERATION AND DEVELOPMENT

The OECD is a unique forum where governments work together to address the economic, social and environmental challenges of globalisation. The OECD is also at the forefront of efforts to understand and to help governments respond to new developments and concerns, such as corporate governance, the information economy and the challenges of an ageing population. The Organisation provides a setting where governments can compare policy experiences, seek answers to common problems, identify good practice and work to co-ordinate domestic and international policies.

The OECD member countries are: Australia, Austria, Belgium, Canada, Chile, the Czech Republic, Denmark, Estonia, Finland, France, Germany, Greece, Hungary, Iceland, Ireland, Israel, Italy, Japan, Korea, Luxembourg, Mexico, the Netherlands, New Zealand, Norway, Poland, Portugal, the Slovak Republic, Slovenia, Spain, Sweden, Switzerland, Turkey, the United Kingdom and the United States. The European Union takes part in the work of the OECD.

OECD Publishing disseminates widely the results of the Organisation's statistics gathering and research on economic, social and environmental issues, as well as the conventions, guidelines and standards agreed by its members.

OECD PUBLISHING, 2, rue André-Pascal, 75775 PARIS CEDEX 16
(962015051P1) ISBN 978-92-64-24590-7-05